A-Z EDINBURGH

CONTENTS

REFERENCE

Motorway	**M8**	Airport	✈
A Road	**A702**	Car Park (Selected)	P
Proposed		Church or Chapel	†
B Road	**B701**	Fire Station	■
Dual Carriageway		Hospital	H
One-way Street		House Numbers A & B Roads only	122 ... 68
Traffic flow on A Roads is also indicated by a heavy line on the driver's left.	⇒	Information Centre	i
Junction Name	GOGAR JUNCTION	National Grid Reference	575
Restricted Access		Park & Ride	Ingliston P+🚌
Pedestrianized Road		Police Station	▲
Track / Footpath		Post Office	★
Residential Walkway		Toilet: without facilities for the disabled	▽
Cycleway		with facilities for the disabled	▽
Railway	Level Crossing / Station / Tunnel	Viewpoint	⁎ ☀
Built-up Area	MILL LA	Educational Establishment	
Local Authority Boundary	— · — · —	Hospital or Hospice	
Posttown Boundary		Industrial Building	
Postcode Boundary within Posttown	— ·· — ·· —	Leisure or Recreational Facility	
		Place of Interest	
Map Continuation	8 Large Scale Centre 4	Public Building	
		Shopping Centre or Market	
		Other Selected Buildings	

SCALE

Map Pages 6-50	1:19000 3.33 inches to 1 mile
0 ¼ ½ Mile	
0 250 500 750 Metres	
5.26cm to 1km 8.47cm to 1 mile	

Map Pages 4-5	1:9500 6.7 inches to 1 mile
0 ⅛ ¼ Mile	
0 125 250 375 Metres	
10.52cm to 1km 16.94 cm to 1 mile	

Copyright of Geographers' A-Z Map Company Limited

Head Office :
Fairfield Road, Borough Green, Sevenoaks, Kent TN15 8PP
Telephone: 01732 781000 (Enquiries & Trade Sales)
            01732 783422 (Retail Sales)
www.a-zmaps.co.uk

Ordnance Survey®

Copyright © Geographers' A-Z Map Co. Ltd.

© Crown Copyright

EDITION 4 2005

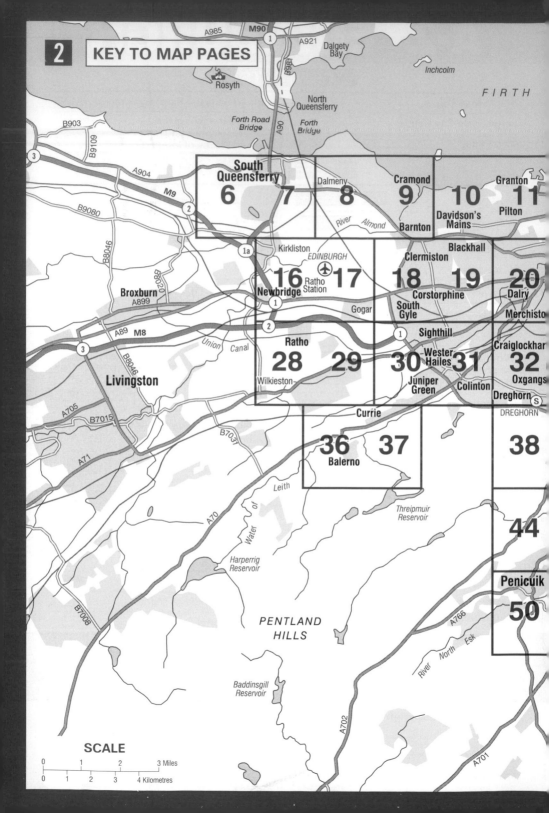

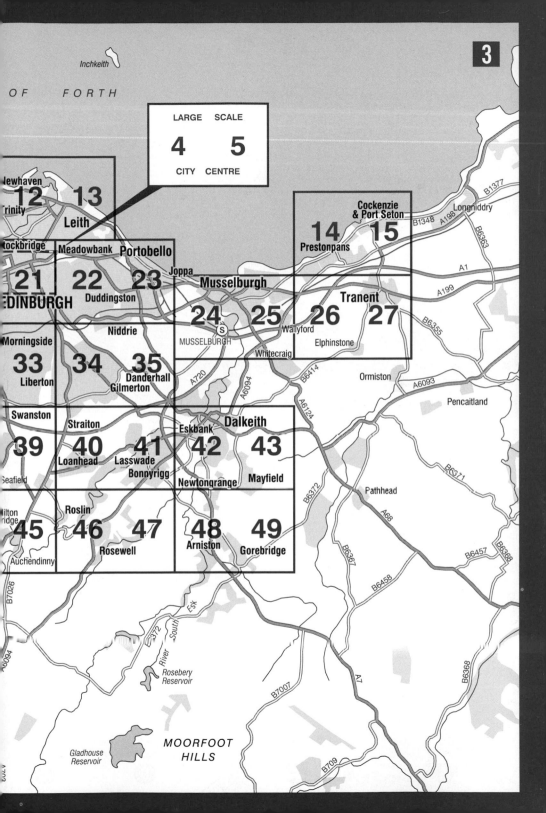

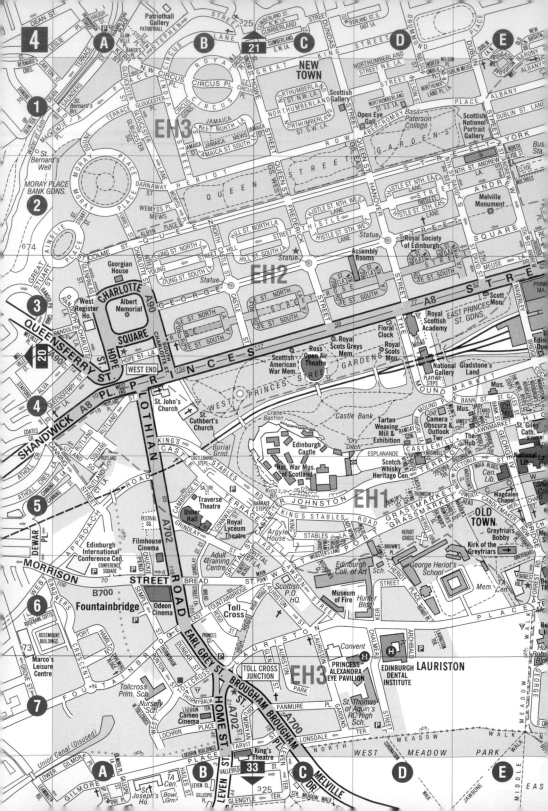

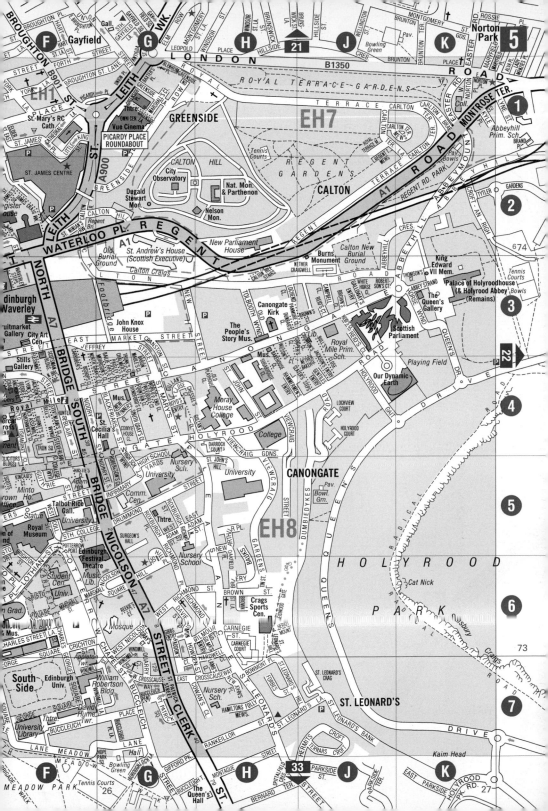

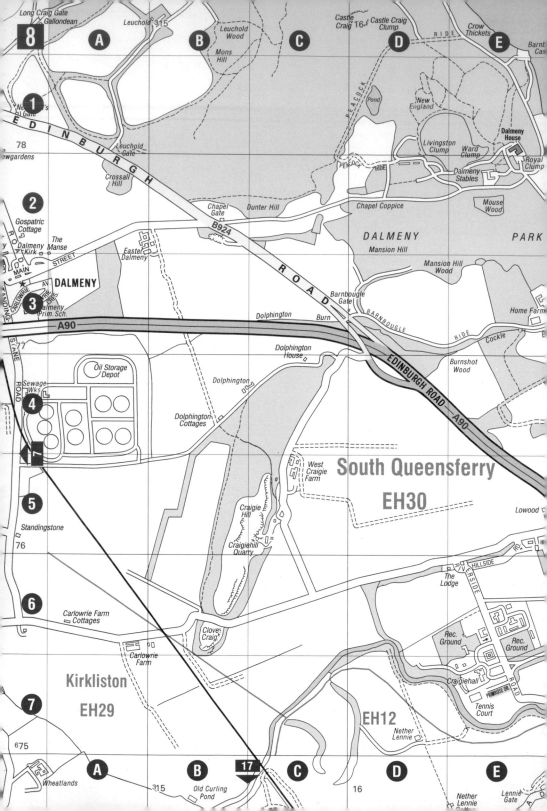

8

A   B   C   D   E

Long Craig Gate
Gallondean
Leuchold 315
Leuchold Wood
Mons Hill
Castle Craig 16.6
Castle Craig Clump
Crow Thickets
Barnb Cas

1
New's Gate
Pond
New England
Dalmeny House

78
EDINBURGH
Leuchold Gate
Livingston Clump
Ward Clump
Dalmeny Stables
Royal Clump
Crossall Hill

2
Gospatric Cottage
Chapel Gate
Dunter Hill
Chapel Coppice
Mouse Wood
The Manse
Dalmeny Kirk
B924
Easter Dalmeny
DALMENY
DALMENY PARK
Mansion Hill
Mansion Hill Wood

3
Dalmeny Prim. Sch.
A90
Dolphington Burn
Barnbougle Gate
BARNBOUGLE
Home Farm
Dolphington House
RIDE
Cockle

Oil Storage Depot
Dolphington
Burnshot Wood
EDINBURGH ROAD A90

4
Sewage Wks
77
Dolphington Cottages
West Craigie Farm
South Queensferry
EH30

7
Craigie Hill
Lowood

5
Standingstone
76
Craigiehill Quarry
RIVERSIDE
HILLSIDE
The Lodge

6
Carlowrie Farm Cottages
Cloves Craig
Rec. Ground
Rec. Ground
Craigiehall

Carlowrie Farm
Tennis Court

7
Kirkliston
EH29
PENROSE DR
Nether Lennie
EH12

675
Wheatlands
315
Old Curling Pond
17
16
Nether Lennie
Lennie Gate

A   B   C   D   E

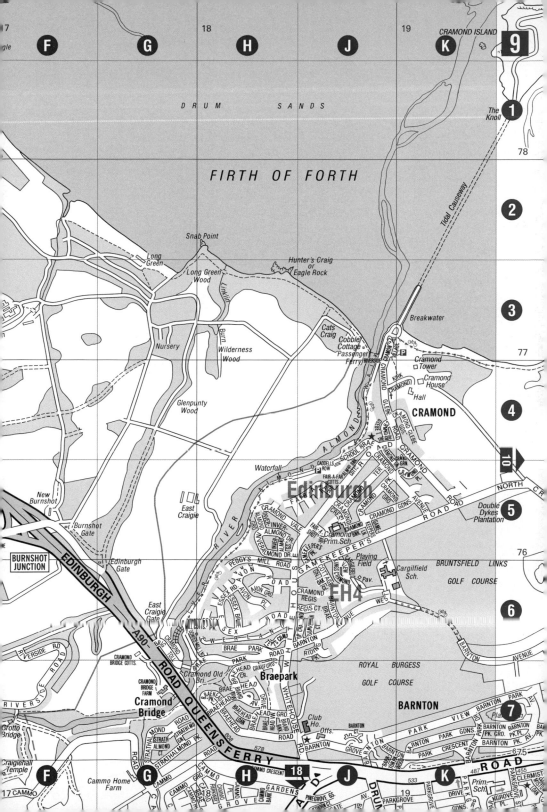

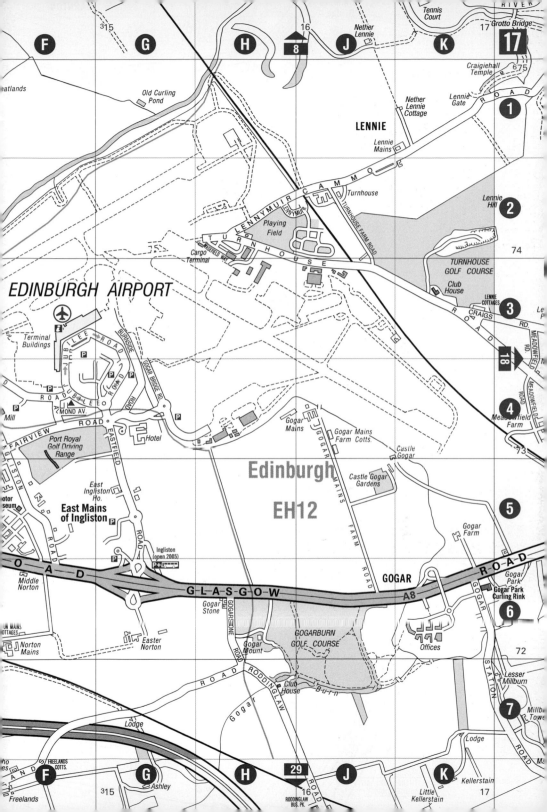

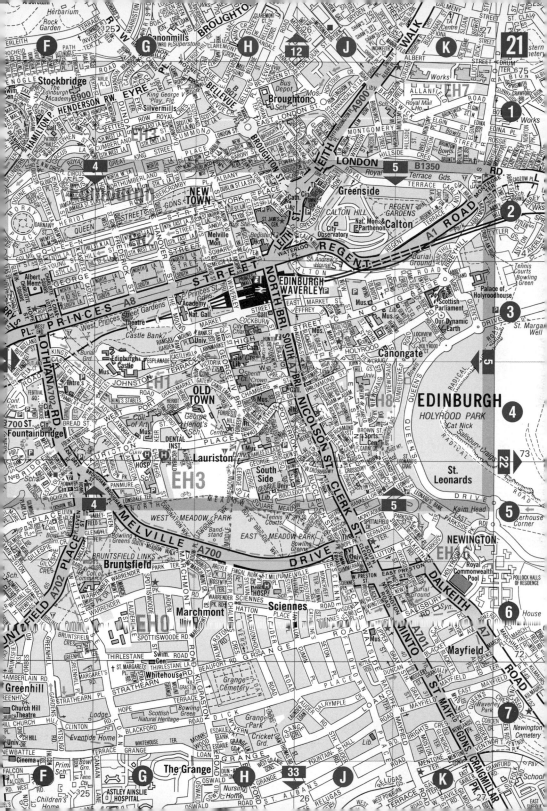

Musselburgh

EH21

Prestonpans

EH32

ROYAL MUSSELBURGH
GOLF COURSE

A199

A1 MUSSELBURGH

BY-PASS

TRANENT

A199

Drummohr Caravan Park

Drum-Mohr

Wallyford Toll

Dolphingston Toll

East Lodge

West Lodge

Dolphingstone Farm

Club House

South Lodge

Prestongrange Ind. Heritage Mus.

Visitor Cen.

Morrison's Haven Exhibition Hall

Ravenshaugh Burn

Bowl Grn. Pav.

Comm. Cen. Rec. Grd.

WALLYFORD INDUSTRIAL ESTATE

St. Clement's Wells

WHINNY

LOAN

Falside Hill

Myles Farm

Falside Castle

West Mains

Colton Dean

Football Grd. Pav.

Hall

Crookston Rd

Elphinstone Twr. Farm Cottages

Elphinstone Tower

B6414

Carberry Hill

Hillhead Farm

Prestonpan

Rigley Hill

Bankhead

Birsley Brae

MID MID ROAD IND. EST.

JOHNNIE

LOPES ROAD

B1361

A6094

73

71

670

37

38

39

14

38

37

39

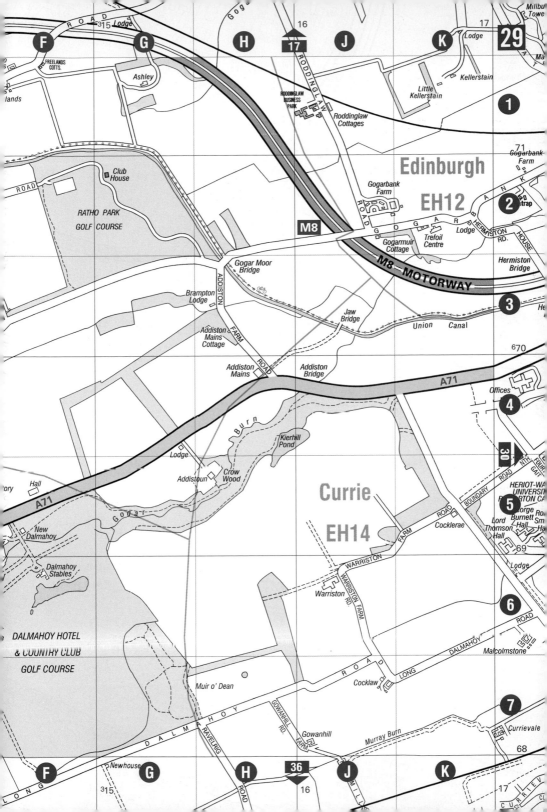

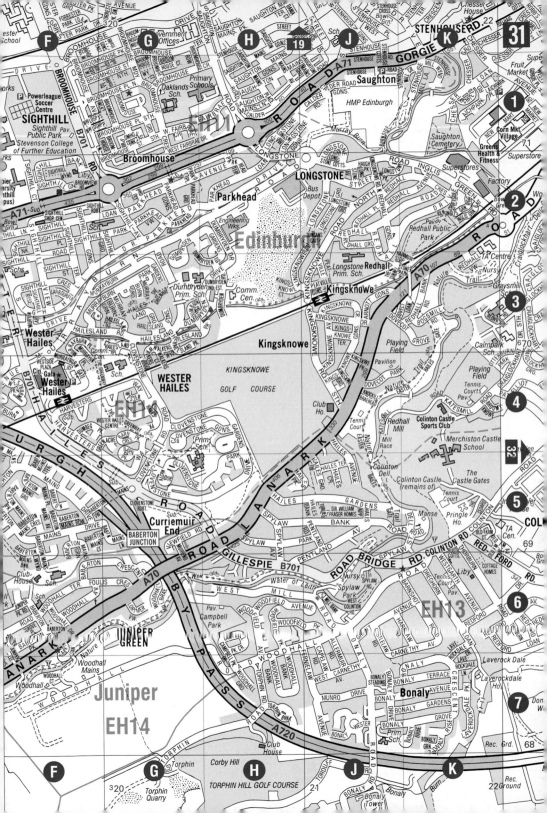

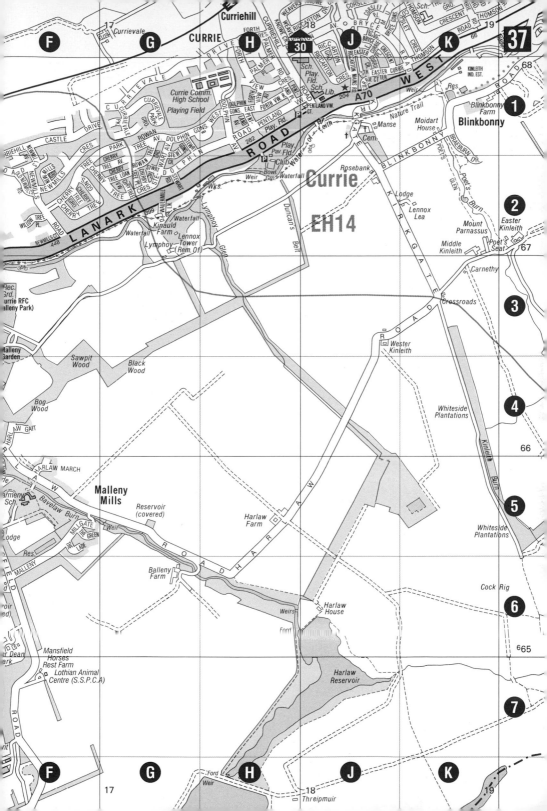

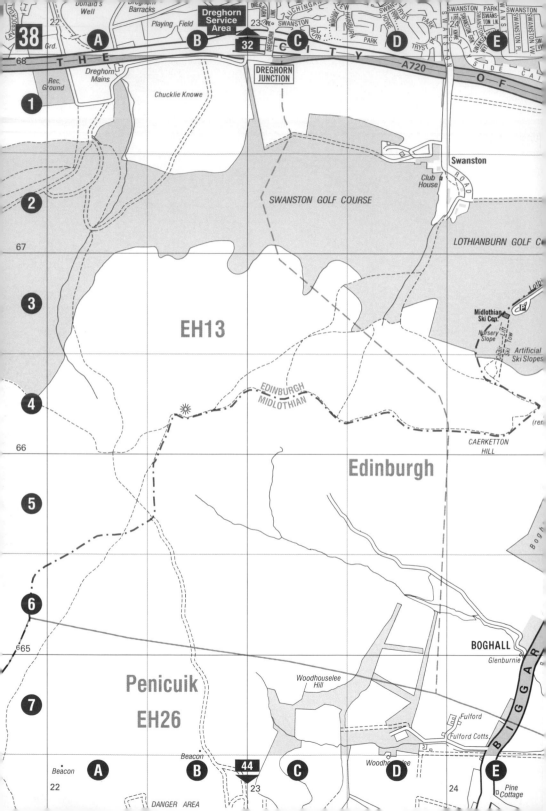

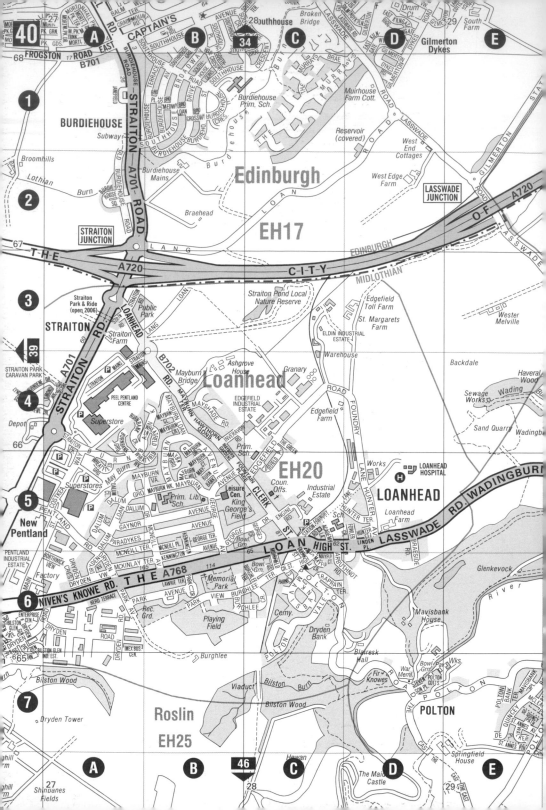

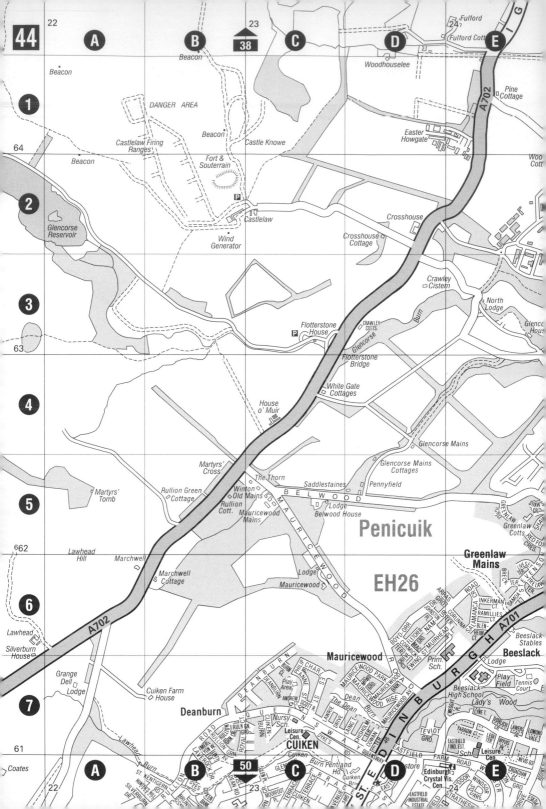

GUIDE TO SELECTED PLACES OF INTEREST

HOW TO USE THE GUIDE

Opening times for places of interest vary considerably depending on the season, day of the week or the ownership of the property. Please check opening times before starting your journey.

The index reference is to the square in which the place of interest appears. e.g. **Arthur's Seat** 5B **22**, is to be found in square 5B on page 22.

HS, Historic Scotland - Always open.
NTS, National Trust of Scotland - Always open.
NTS, National Trust of Scotland - Restricted opening.

EDINBURGH

Referred to as the 'Athens of the North', Edinburgh is a flourishing city renowned for its history, style, diversity, and prestigious annual festival, which is considered to be the most important and successful event of its kind in Britain. During the month of August, the city becomes a magnet for thousands of people from around the world intent on participating in the festival scene.

Edinburgh divides itself between the Old and New Town areas. The Old Town includes the ancient city centre, where the famous Royal Mile links the Castle and Holyrood, and the historical districts of Grassmarket and Greyfriars. The New Town, dating mainly from the 18th century extends north from Princes Street, Edinburgh's main shopping street, and comprises a continuous development of grand streets, squares, circuses and green spaces regarded as a masterpiece of urban architecture.

 Tourist Information Centre (All year):
3 Princes Street. Tel: 0845 22 55 121

www.edinburgh.org

Arthur's Seat   5B **22**

The remnant of a volcanic eruption dating back to the Carboniferous period, this natural attraction is a prominent and celebrated landmark of the city skyline. Positioned within Holyrood Park to the east of the city centre, it stands at just 250m (823 feet) and is easily surmountable in an hour by way of its gentle slopes. A breath-taking panoramic view of Edinburgh's magnificent cityscape awaits those who reach the summit, and if attempted on a clear day, the mountains of the Trossachs can be seen.

Bank of Scotland Museum   4E **4**

This innovative museum reflects the 300 year history of Scotland's first bank. Displays include early adding machines, bank notes, forgeries, gold coins and photographs.

Brass Rubbing Centre
(Chalmers Close)   4G **5**

Housed in Trinity Apse, the only remaining part of the collegiate church founded in 1462. The centre holds a fine collection of replica brasses and Pictish stones from which rubbings can be made.

Britannia   3E **12**

The decommissioning of Britannia as a working royal yacht has allowed visitors an insight into the splendour of life aboard this illustrious vessel. Highlights of the tour through the decks include the bridge - the hub of the ship, the Admiral's cabin and quarters, the Sun Lounge - reputed to be one of the Queen's favourite places onboard, the State dining and drawing rooms, and the Queen and Duke of Edinburgh's bedrooms. A fascinating glimpse into a piece of royal history.

Burns Monument   2J **5**

A monument dedicated to Scotland's most beloved poet Robert Burns (1759-1796) built in 1830 by architect Thomas Hamilton.

Butterfly and Insect World   1J **41**

A popular attraction housed in a vast indoor rainforest. Visitors experience the free-flying butterflies first-hand, while the daily 'Meet the Beasties' sessions allow for close handling of the more friendlier creatures. Tarantulas, leaf-cutting ants, scorpions, pythons and chameleons are also part of the experience.

Calton Hill   2G **5**

Although Calton Hill may not be the highest of the city's hills, it still enjoys the most spectacular outlook with views stretching to Leith and the Firth of Forth to the north, and Holyrood Park to the south. The most distinguishing feature by far must be the unusual assortment of buildings and monuments dotted about the vicinity, in particular, the National Monument - a tribute to the Parthenon, and the Nelson Monument - built in the shape of a telescope.

Camera Obscura — 4D 4

Dating from 1850, this 'cinema' offers a unique panoramic history of Edinburgh; as the lights dim, a moving image of the surrounding city is projected and as the mirror revolves the past is revealed. Paintings and photographs of life in the city between 1780 and 1900 are displayed and there is an exhibition of 3-D Holography.

Childhood Museum — 4G 5

This museum houses an extensive collection of childhood memorabilia including toys, games, books and dolls. For the adult visitor there are exhibitions relating to the history of child welfare including health, education and upbringing.

City Art Centre (2 Market Street) — 3F 5

A rich collection of fine art, almost entirely by Scottish artists, is housed within the City Art Centre. Since opening in 1980, the six exhibition galleries have displayed work dating from the 17th century, encompassing a wide range of media, including painting, drawing, print, sculpture, tapestry and photography.

Craigmillar Castle — 2D 34

A beautifully preserved medieval castle seated 3 miles south east from the city centre. Its historical significance is undoubtedly linked to Mary, Queen of Scots who sought refuge in its walls after the infamous murder of her secretary, David Rizzio, at Holyrood Palace. The castle also bore witness to the plot to assassinate Mary's second husband, the brutish Lord Darnley.

Dalmeny House — 1E 8

The stately home of the Earls of Rosebery for over 300 years, Dalmeny House is an interesting mix of Tudor revival, with its octagonal towers and carved chimneys, gothic flourishes of stained glass and fan vaulted corridors, and lavish rooms in typical Regency style. Paintings by Gainsborough, Raeburn, Reynolds and Lawrence adorn the walls of the Dining room, while Scotland's premier collection of French tapestries, porcelain and furniture occupy other rooms. A notable hallmark of this house is the collection of Napoleonic accoutrements, from paintings of the Emperor, to personal furniture and mementoes amassed by Prime Minister Archibald Philip Primrose, 5th Earl of Rosebery.

Dean Gallery — 3D 20

Noted for its impressive collections of Dada and Surrealism, the Dean Gallery also boasts an extensive body of work by Edinburgh-born sculptor Sir Eduardo Paolozzi including drawings, prints, plaster maquettes, and artefacts from his studio donated by the artist himself. Located opposite the Scottish National Gallery of Modern Art, the gallery's grounds play host to sculpture by Bourdelle, Hamilton, Finlay, Turnbull, Rickey and Paolozzi. Visitors can also view items from the gallery library and archive by appointment.

Edinburgh Castle HS — 4C 4

The imposing fortress of Edinburgh Castle has dominated the cityscape since the Middle Ages, defiantly rooted to the ancient volcanic outcrop upon which it stands. Far from being a quaint romantic vision of a castle, its strategic positioning and defensive structure have withstood countless sieges, and provided successive Kings and Queens with refuge in times of peril. Mary, Queen of Scots, chose to give birth to her son, James VI of Scotland (James I of England upon the death of Elizabeth I) within its safe confines, and the tiny room in which this took place can be seen by visitors today. It was James IV that commissioned the striking hammerbeam roof in the Great Hall, with the castle's principal courtyard, the Crown Square, developed sometime in the 16th century. Of particular note is the remarkable St Margaret's Chapel, which has remained perfectly intact for 900 years, making it Edinburgh's oldest surviving building. Unearthed in 1818 by Sir Walter Scott, the crown jewels lay dormant for over a hundred years in a locked room in the depths of the castle. These treasured symbols of royalty, known as the Honours of Scotland, comprising the Crown, Sceptre and Sword of State, are now viewable by the pubic, together with the Stone of Destiny, the One o'clock Gun and the famous 15th century siege gun Mons Meg.

Edinburgh Crystal (Eastfield, Penicuik) — 1D 50

Visitors to the working factory can witness the skilled craftsmen at work, sample the elaborate art of glassblowing and take a a look at multimedia exhibits detailing how the renowned crystal is made.

Edinburgh Dungeon — 3E 4

Experience life in barbaric times through reconstructions, exhibits and special effects that evoke the horrific aspect of Scotland's past. Relive the devastation of the plague, inspect gruesome torture devices and discover the brutal reality of clan warfare.

Edinburgh Experience 2G 5
(City Observatory, Calton Hill)

Located in the City Observatory on Calton Hill, a fascinating 3-D multimedia tour of Edinburgh awaits visitors to this rewarding attraction. Learn how Scotland's capital evolved from its volcanic ancestry to become a city of culture and beauty.

Edinburgh University Collection of Historic Musical Instruments
(Reid Concert Hall, Bristo Square) 6E 4

An outstanding and diverse collection of over 1000 musical instruments from around the world chronicling the art of instrument making over the past 400 years. On display are some fine examples of wind, string, brass and percussion instruments.

Edinburgh Zoo 4H 19

In the Corstorphine area of Edinburgh lies one of Scotland's top tourist attractions. The zoo is inhabited by 1,000 animals from over 150 species ranging from Meer Cats and Snow Leopards, to King Penguins and Dwarf Crocodiles. Watch out for the daily Penguin parade and activities such as Sealion feeding and the hilltop safari.

Fire, Museum of 6C 4

Displays illustrate the history of the oldest municipal fire brigade in the UK. Other exhibits include fire engines dating from 1806 and information relating to the development of fire fighting.

Edinburgh Festival

Every year, for six weeks starting in late July, the city throws open its doors and streets to host a myriad of cultural events, comprising theatre, comedy, cinema, music, literature and military expertise. Recognised the world-over as one of the most acclaimed celebrations of the arts, it is certainly a most stimulating and enjoyable experience for both participant and visitor alike.

Founded back in 1947, the original line-up of events consisted of the Edinburgh International Festival, the Fringe Festival, and the International Film Festival. It was hoped that in a post war world it would re-unite people and provide some much needed merriment. By 1950, the addition of the Military Tattoo allowed the Army to demonstrate their skill and pageantry, while in more recent times the Edinburgh Book Festival, and Edinburgh Jazz and Blues Festival have emerged as successful events.

Edinburgh International Festival
From its inception in the late 1940's, the International Festival has attracted the world's eminent performing arts companies, from such disciplines as theatre, opera, ballet, and music. Considered to be the more highbrow of the festivals, it is staged in various venues around the city, with the beauty of Edinburgh's architecture enhancing each performance with a most unique atmosphere.

The Fringe Festival
Proud of its all-embracing, avant-garde approach to performance, the Fringe grew out of an impulsive grass roots reaction to the more conventional International Festival. Reflecting its 'open access' principle, the festival showcases the talent of students and professionals alike, from lively amateur productions to stand-up comedy, and small-scale productions to West End dramatics.

Edinburgh International Film Festival
While Cannes may be more synonymous with film, Edinburgh's International Film Festival has grown in stature since 1947 to become the world's longest continually running celebration of cinema. Its reputation as a most worthy and successful event has encouraged the growth of the British film industry and provided a platform for new and inspiring filmmaking.

Edinburgh Military Tattoo
For over fifty years the tattoo has been an annual event staged in the dramatic setting of the Castle Esplanade. Garnering a reputation for unrivalled pageantry and skill, the programme is timed to coincide with twilight to silhouette the breathtaking backdrop of Edinburgh Castle. Although the performances vary year on year, the show inevitably features the music of the massed Pipes and Drums of the Scottish Regiments and Military Bands and a lone piper performing from the battlements. Televised in 30 countries amassing 100 million viewers, the event has welcomed international participants from as far afield as Nepal and New Zealand. The finale is naturally an awesome climax to events with the gathering of the performers for the taking of the salute, together with a dazzling fireworks display.

Floral Clock 3D 4

In 1903, John McHattie, the city's park superintendent, conceived the idea of the Floral Clock. Imitated by many cities around the world, the face and hands of the working clock are carpeted with thousands of small hardy plants, all of which have to be replanted every spring. Each year this new display adopts a topical theme publicising a particular event or organisation. Be sure to arrive in time for the quaint cuckoo that announces every quarter past the hour.

Forth Bridge 1F 7

The imposing cantilever bridge, spanning 1.5 miles, stands as testament to robust engineering from the Industrial Age. It remains one of the most distinctive landmarks in Scotland, carrying trains over the Firth of Forth.

Fruitmarket Gallery, The 3F 5

Exhibiting a changing programme of contemporary art, the former market venue has featured work by such major figures as Bill Viola, James Turrell, Yoko Ono and Gerhard Richter, while still providing a platform for established and emerging Scottish artists.

Georgian House, The NTS 3A 4

Situated on the north side of Charlotte Square, this house designed by Robert Adam in 1796 exemplifies the style of Edinburgh's New Town architecture. The rooms of number 7 are furnished in period style and there is a video presentation that reflects life in the New Town. The National Trust for Scotland also owns numbers 5 and 6 on the north side and 26 to 31 on the south.

Gladstone's Land NTS 4E 4

Built in 1620, this six-storey tenement building in the Old Town is furnished in period style with unusual tempera paintings on the ceilings and walls.

Greyfriars Bobby 5E 4

Statue in memory of Greyfriars Bobby, the Skye terrier who watched over his master's grave for 14 years after his death from 1858 to 1872.

Holyrood Abbey HS 3K 5

The ruined nave is all that remains of this once magnificent Abbey church, founded for Augustinian canons during the late 12th early 13th centuries. A substantial amount of the building was destroyed in the Reformation and, sadly, attempts to restore the ruin in the 18th century were abandoned when the roof collapsed. Beneath the Abbey the Royal Vault is the final resting place for a number of Scottish Kings, including David II (son of Robert the Bruce), James II, James V and Lord Darnley, Mary Queen of Scot's second husband.

Inverleith House 5E 4

Set within the heart of the Royal Botanic Gardens, the gallery at Inverleith House boasts notable sculptural work by Andy Goldsworthy and Barbara Hepworth. Past exhibitions have featured artists such as Damien Hirst, Callum Innes, Simon Starling and Carl Andre.

John Knox House (43-45 High Street) 4G 5

There is some contention as to whether John Knox, the religious reformer, actually lived in this 15th century town house. It is known, however, that it was once inhabited by James Mossman, goldsmith to Mary, Queen of Scots. Maintained by the Church of Scotland, the house features relics of the Reformation and information regarding Knox's life and influence.

Lauriston Castle 5B 10

Near to the southern side of the Firth of Forth stands this 16th century Tower House. Much altered in the 19th century to include Jacobean style features, in 1926 Lauriston Castle was left in trust to the nation by its last private owners Mr and Mrs William Robert Reid. The original Edwardian interiors remain, and showcase some fine examples of period furniture, Flemish tapestries and Derbyshire Blue John ware.

Malleny Garden NTS 3F 37

Maintained by the National Trust for Scotland, this pleasant walled garden allows visitors to enjoy the beautiful collection of old-fashioned roses and herbaceous borders. Of particular note is the quartet of clipped yew trees that date back 400 years. Additionally, the National Bonsai Collection for Scotland is located here.

Matthew Architecture Gallery, The 5E 4
(20 Chambers Street)

Since opening in 1992, the gallery has exhibited examples of historical and contemporary architecture, together with expositions from internationally acclaimed architects.

Museum of Edinburgh, The 3H 5

Huntly House, a beautifully well-preserved 16th

century building, provides the setting for exhibitions devoted to the local history of Edinburgh. The diverse range of artefacts include pottery, silverware, street signs and treasures of national importance, such as the National Covenant and articles related to Field Marshal Earl Haig.

Museum of Scotland   5E 4

A prominent and impressive building in Edinburgh's diverse cityscape, the Museum serves to recount the story of Scotland with reference to its geology, the history of its people and their culture.

National Gallery of Scotland   4D 4

Located in the heart of the city, the gallery has been open to the public since 1859. The collection comprises a comprehensive catalogue of work from the Renaissance era to the Post Impressionist period.

National Library of Scotland   4E 4

Founded in 1682, the library is one of the largest in Britain and since 1710 has been able to claim a copy of every book published in Britain.

National Monument   2H 5

Built in 1822 to honour the Scottish who perished in the Napoleonic wars, this monument was designed to emulate the Parthenon, (temple dedicated to Athena, the Greek goddess of War). Unfortunately, it was never completed due to a collapse in funding and remains today unfinished.

National War Museum of Scotland   5C 4
(Edinburgh Castle)

The history of Scotland cannot be told without reference to war and military service, and its effect on its people and their land. This absorbing museum reflects the experience of war, sourced from personal diaries, photographs and official documents. Other exhibits include uniforms, insignia and equipment, medals, decorations, weapons, paintings, ceramics and silverware.

Nelson Monument   2H 5

Built between 1807 and 1815, this was one of the first monuments to Admiral Nelson. The climb to the top is rewarded with splendid panoramic views across the city.

Newhailes NTS   2B 24

An outstanding 17th century house characterised by its original rococo interiors and curious landscape.

Built in 1686 and added to in the 18th century, the building once held an impressive collection of books in its library (later moved to the National Library of Scotland) and was described by Dr Samuel Johnson as "the most learned room in Europe". Now in the hands of The National Trust for Scotland, the grounds have undergone archaeological investigations, which have revealed some remarkable features - a raised walkway, water garden with cascades and a rococo shell grotto.

Our Dynamic Earth   4J 5

This highly stimulating interactive centre uses the latest interpretative technology to take the visitor on a journey of discovery of Earth's evolution from the 'Big Bang' to the present day. Experience extreme environments from the rumbling of an earthquake to the torrential downpour of a tropical rainstorm. Awarded a grant from the Millennium Commission, Our Dynamic Earth is Scotland's largest new visitor attraction.

Palace of Holyroodhouse
& Holyrood Park   3K 5

At the opposite end of the Royal Mile, providing a 'bookend' with Edinburgh Castle, stands the fine baroque Palace of Holyroodhouse, and its adjoining royal parkland. Steeped in history, with its origins dating back to 1128, it is most commonly associated with Mary, Queen of Scots, who spent six tumultuous years within its walls from 1561. Subsequent Kings and Queens, including Queen Elizabeth II, have used the palace as their official Royal residence in Scotland. Today, tourists can visit the Royal apartments, the Throne room, the Royal Dining Room and the Great Gallery to experience the grandeur of this historical address. Holyrood Park, some 630 acres of unique landscape, contains an array of wonders; from the panoramic vista of the ancient Arthur's Seat, to the numerous holy wells dotted around the park.

People's Story, The   3H 5

Housed in the 16th century Tolbooth, this museum reflects working class life in Edinburgh since the 18th century. Sounds, sights, smells and reconstructed rooms combine to evoke an atmosphere of a bygone era.

Royal Botanic Garden   7A 12

Established in 1670, the garden is considered to be one of the finest in the world, covering over 6% of the plant kingdom. "The Botanics", as it is locally known, covers seventy acres with features such as the Temperate Palm House, arranged into ten climate

zones and, at 23 metres high, is the UK's tallest Palm House - a definite must-see. A visit to the Peat and Rock House showcases the world's largest collection of Vireya Rhododendrons, while the tranquil setting of the Chinese Hillside provides visitors with the chance to see some historic Chinese species. A thoroughly rewarding and exhilarating experience.

Royal Museum   5F 5

Housed in a most impressive Victorian building designed by Capt. Francis Fowkes, the architect of the Royal Albert Hall in London, the museum's diverse collection covers natural history, geology, science and technology, and decorative arts. From whale skeletons to steamships, black holes to classical Greek sculptures, minerals and fossils to totem poles, there is sure to be something to amaze everyone.

Royal Scottish Academy   3D 4

Scotland's oldest gallery dedicated to the display of contemporary art. Exhibitions include all styles of work within this genre from college students to associates of the Royal Academy.

St. Giles' Cathedral   4E 4

Founded in 1120, most of the remaining architecture dates from the 14th and 15th centuries, including the famous crown spire that dominates the city skyline. Also known as the High Kirk of Edinburgh, it contains the Chapel of the Order of the Thistle (Scotland's chivalric company of Knights) and is also noted for its stained glass windows that date from the 1870's onwards.

St. Mary's RC Cathedral   1F 5

The Cathedral church of St Mary was designed by Gillespie Graham and dates from 1814 and 1890. The St Andrews Altar contains the National Shrine to Scotland's patron saint.

Scotch Whisky Heritage Centre   5D 4

An award winning attraction that takes the visitor on a ride through history in a whisky barrel to discover the ancient traditions and origins of whisky production.

Scottish National Gallery of Modern Art   3C 20

A fine collection of 19th and 20th century artwork resides in this exceptional gallery set in parkland to the west of the city centre. Treasured work by such notable figures as Matisse, Picasso, Bacon, Hockney, Warhol, and Moore sit comfortably amid light and spacious surroundings. A deserving aspect of the

gallery is the presence of work by Scottish artists Mackintosh, the Scottish Colourists, Gillies, Maxwell, Eardley, to name but a few.

Scottish Parliament   3K 5

Standing boldly at the foot of the historic Royal Mile, the new parliament building allows visitors to explore its public galleries of the chamber and committee rooms, watch proceedings from information screens in the main hall and discover the history behind the Scottish Parliament through exhibitions.

Scott Monument   3E 4

One of Edinburgh's most famous landmarks, this monument to Sir Walter Scott was designed by George Kemp and erected between 1840 and 1844. The statue itself depicts Scott with his dog and incorporates characters from his novels.

Scottish National Portrait Gallery   1E 4

Visual history of Scotland from the 16th century to the present day depicted through portraits of figures that shaped it: royalty, philosophers, poets and rebels are included. The gallery also houses the National Collection of Photography.

Stills Gallery   4F 5

Scotland's premier photographic gallery exhibits a generous collection of contemporary photography.

Talbot Rice Gallery   5F 5

The gallery exhibits Edinburgh University's 'Old Master' collection alongside a changing programme of temporary displays.

Tartan Weaving Mill and Exhibition   4D 4

Housed in the former Castlehill Reservoir Cistern, this working mill allows visitors to view the entire production process of tartan from sheep to shop.

Water of Leith
(Visitors Centre - 24 Lanark road)   (2A 32)

Once serving as a power supply to a series of mills dating from the 13th century, this picturesque little river flows from its source in the Pentland Hills, winding through the centre of Edinburgh to its mouth with the Firth of Forth, covering 35km in all. The Water of Leith Walkway trails the course of the river over 19km from Balerno to Leith, with a well-equipped visitor centre located halfway at Slateford. Visitors can learn more about the heritage and wildlife associated with this charming waterway through interactive exhibitions.

INDEX

Including Streets, Places & Areas, Hospitals & Hospices, Industrial Estates,
Selected Flats & Walkways, Stations, Junctions and Selected Places of Interest.

HOW TO USE THIS INDEX

1. Each street name is followed by its Postcode District and then by its Locality abbreviation(s) and then by its map reference;
e.g. **Abbey Rd.** EH22: Dalk . . . .3B **42** is in the EH22 Postcode District and the Dalkeith Locality and is to be found in square 3B on page **42**.
The page number is shown in bold type.

2. A strict alphabetical order is followed in which Av., Rd., St., etc. (though abbreviated) are read in full and as part of the street name;
e.g. **Almondside** appears after **Almond Rd.** but before **Almond Sq.**

3. Streets and a selection of flats and walkways too small to be shown on the maps, appear in the index with the thoroughfare to which it is connected shown in brackets; e.g. **Abbeyhill Ind. Est.** EH8: Edin . . . .2A **22** (off Abbey La.)

4. Addresses that are in more than one part are referred to as not continuous.

5. Places and areas are shown in the index in BLUE TYPE and the map reference is to the actual map square in which the town centre or area is located and not to the place name shown on the map; e.g. BALERNO 4E **36**

6. An example of a selected place of interest is **Edinburgh Castle** 4C **4**

7. An example of a station is **Brunstane Station (Rail)** 5J **23**

8. Junction names and Service Areas are shown in the index in BOLD TYPE; e.g. BABERTON JUNC. 5G **31**

9. An example of a hospital is ASTLEY AINSLIE HOSPITAL 1G **33**

10. Map references shown in brackets; e.g. **Abbeyhill** EH8: Edin . . . .3K **21** (3K **5**) refer to entries that also appear on the large scale pages **4-5**.

GENERAL ABBREVIATIONS

App. : Approach	**Cres.** : Crescent	**La.** : Lane	**Rdbt.** : Roundabout
Arc. : Arcade	**Cft.** : Croft	**Lit.** : Little	**Shop.** : Shopping
Av. : Avenue	**Dr.** : Drive	**Lwr.** : Lower	**Sth.** : South
Bk. : Back	**E.** : East	**Mnr.** : Manor	**Sq.** : Square
Bri. : Bridge	**Est.** : Estate	**Mkt.** : Market	**Sta.** : Station
B'way. : Broadway	**Fld.** : Field	**Mdw.** : Meadow	**St.** : Street
Bldgs. : Buildings	**Gdn.** : Garden	**M.** : Mews	**Ter.** : Terrace
Bus. : Business	**Gdns.** : Gardens	**Mt.** : Mount	**Twr.** : Tower
Cvn. : Caravan	**Ga.** : Gate	**Mus.** : Museum	**Trad.** : Trading
C'way. : Causeway	**Gt.** : Great	**Nth.** : North	**Up.** : Upper
Cen. : Centre	**Grn.** : Green	**Pde.** : Parade	**Va.** : Vale
Chu. : Church	**Gro.** : Grove	**Pk.** : Park	**Vw.** : View
Circ. : Circle	**Hgts.** : Heights	**Pav.** : Pavilion	**Vs.** : Villas
Cir. : Circus	**Ho.** : House	**Pl.** : Place	**Vis.** : Visitors
Cl. : Close	**Ho's.** : Houses	**Quad.** : Quadrant	**Wlk.** : Walk
Cnr. : Corner	**Ind.** : Industrial	**Res.** : Residential	**W.** : West
Cotts. : Cottages	**Info.** : Information	**Ri.** : Rise	**Yd.** : Yard
Ct. : Court	**Junc.** : Junction	**Rd.** : Road	

LOCALITY ABBREVIATIONS

Auch : **Auchendinny**	Edin : **Edinburgh**	May : **Mayfield**	Rat S : **Ratho Station**
Bal : **Balerno**	Edin A : **Edinburgh Airport**	Mil B : **Milton Bridge**	Rose : **Rosewell**
Bil : **Bilston**	Elph : **Elphinstone**	Muss : **Musselburgh**	Rosl : **Roslin**
Bonn : **Bonnyrigg**	Gore : **Gorebridge**	Nbdge : **Newbridge**	S Q'fry : **South Queensferry**
Cock : **Cockenzie**	Ing : **Ingliston**	Newh : **Newhaven**	Tran : **Tranent**
Cram : **Cramond**	J Grn : **Juniper Green**	Newt : **Newtongrange**	Wall : **Wallyford**
Cur : **Currie**	Kltn : **Kirkliston**	Pen : **Penicuik**	Whit : **Whitecraig**
Dalk : **Dalkeith**	Kntn : **Kirknewton**	Port : **Portobello**	Wilk : **Wilkieston**
Dalm : **Dalmeny**	Las : **Lasswade**	Port S : **Port Seton**	Winch : **Winchburgh**
Dan : **Danderhall**	Leith : **Leith**	Pres : **Prestonpans**	
East : **Easthouses**	Loan : **Loanhead**	Rat : **Ratho**	

A

A1 Ind. Pk. EH15: Port 4H **23**
ABBEYHILL 2A **22**
Abbeyhill EH8: Edin 3K **21** (3K **5**)
Abbeyhill Cres.
EH8: Edin 2K **21** (3J **5**)
Abbeyhill Ind. Est. EH8: Edin 2A **22**
(off Abbey La.)
Abbey La. EH8: Edin 2A **22**
Abbeymount EH7: Edin . . .2K **21** (2K **5**)
Abbey Rd. EH22: Dalk 3B **42**
Abbey Strand
EH8: Edin 3K **21** (3K **5**)
Abbey St. EH7: Edin 2A **22**
Abbotsford Ct. EH10: Edin 7E **20**
Abbotsford Cres. EH10: Edin 7E **20**
Abbotsford Pk. EH10: Edin 7E **20**
Abercorn Av. EH8: Edin 3D **22**
Abercorn Cotts. EH15: Edin 5D **22**
Abercorn Ct. EH8: Edin 4D **22**
Abercorn Cres. EH8: Edin 3C **22**

Abercorn Dr. EH8: Edin 3C **22**
Abercorn Gdns. EH8: Edin 2D **22**
Abercorn Gro. EH8: Edin 3C **22**
Abercorn Rd. EH8: Edin 3C **22**
Abercorn Ter. EH15: Port 3H **23**
Abercromby Pl.
EH3: Edin 2G **21** (1D **4**)
Abinger Gdns. EH12: Edin 4B **20**
Academy La. EH20: Loan 5C **40**
Academy Pk. EH6: Edin 6F **13**
Academy St. EH6: Leith 6F **13**
Acheson Dr. EH32: Pres 7C **14**
Acklam Path EH20: Loan 6K **39**
Adam Ferguson Ho.
EH21: Muss 3D **24**
Adam Pottery, The 1F **21**
(off Henderson Row)
Adams Cl. EH13: Edin 6D **32**
Adams Well EH13: Edin 5A **32**
Addiston Cres. EH14: Bal 2E **36**
Addiston Farm Rd.
EH28: Rat 3H **29**
Addiston Gro. EH14: Bal 2D **36**
Addiston Pk. EH14: Bal 2D **36**

Adelphi Gro. EH15: Port 3G **23**
Adelphi Pl. EH15: Port 3G **23**
Admiral Ter. EH10: Edin 6F **21**
Admiralty St. EH6: Newh 4E **12**
Advocate's Cl. EH1: Edin 4E **4**
Affleck Ct. EH12: Edin 3C **18**
Afton Pl. EH5: Edin 5K **11**
Afton Ter. EH5: Edin 5K **11**
Agnew Ter. EH6: Edin 5C **12**
Ainslie Pk. Leisure Cen. 5H **11**
Ainslie Pl. EH3: Edin . . .3E **20** (2A **4**)
Aird's Cl. EH1: Edin 5D **4**
Airlie Pl. EH3: Edin 1G **21**
Aitchison's Cl. EH1: Edin 6C **4**
Aitchison's Pl. EH15: Port 2H **23**
Alan Breck Gdns. EH4: Edin 2F **19**
Albany La. EH1: Edin . . .2H **21** (1E **4**)
Albany St. EH1: Edin . . .2H **21** (1E **4**)
Albany St. La.
EH1: Edin 2H **21** (1E **4**)
Albert Bldgs. EH3: Edin 6B **4**
Albert Cl. EH21: Wall 3K **25**
Albert Cres. EH21: Wall 3K **25**

Albert Memorial 3F **21** (3A **4**)
Albert Pl. EH7: Edin 1J **21**
EH21: Wall 3K **25**
(not continuous)
Albert Rd. EH6: Leith 5C **12**
(not continuous)
Albert St. EH7: Edin 7E **12**
Albert Ter. EH10: Edin 7E **20**
EH21: Muss 2G **25**
Albion Gdns. EH7: Edin 1A **22**
Albion Pl. EH7: Edin 1A **22**
Albion Rd. EH7: Edin 1A **22**
Albion Ter. EH7: Edin 1A **22**
Albyn Pl. EH2: Edin 2A **4**
Alcorn Rigg EH14: Edin 5G **31**
(off Clovenstone Dr.)
Alcorn Sq. EH14: Edin 5G **31**
Alderbank EH26: Pen 3D **50**
Alderbank Gdns. EH11: Edin 7C **20**
Alderbank Pl. EH11: Edin 7C **20**
Alderbank Ter. EH11: Edin 7C **20**
Alder Rd. EH32: Port S 4G **15**
Alemoor Cres. EH7: Edin 7G **13**
Alemoor Pk. EH7: Edin 7G **13**

Alexander Dr.—Bavelaw Cres.

Alexander Dr. EH11: Edin 6A **20**
EH32: Pres 7C **14**
Alexandra Bus. Pk. EH28: Nbdge 6A **16**
Alfred Pl. EH9: Edin 7K **21**
Allanfield EH7: Edin 1K **21**
Allan Pk. EH29: Kltn 1A **16**
Allan Pk. Cres. EH14: Edin 1A **32**
Allan Pk. Dr. EH14: Edin 2A **32**
Allan Pk. Gdns. EH14: Edin 2A **32**
Allan Pk. Loan EH14: Edin 2B **32**
Allan Pk. Rd. EH14: Edin 2A **32**
Allan St. EH4: Edin 1E **20**
Allan Ter. EH22: Dalk 2D **42**
Allermuir Av. EH25: Bil 1J **45**
Allermuir Ct. EH13: Edin 5D **32**
Allermuir Rd. EH13: Edin 6J **31**
Allison Pl. EH29: Kltn 1B **16**
Alloway Loan EH16: Edin 3A **34**
Almond Av. EH12: Edin A 4F **17**
Almond Bank Cotts. EH4: Cram 5J **9**
Almondbank Ter. EH11: Edin 7C **20**
Almond Ct. EH16: Edin 1E **34**
Almond Ct. E. *EH4: Cram 7H 9 (off Braehead Pk.)*
Almond Ct. W. *EH4: Cram 7H 9 (off Braehead Pk.)*
Almond Cres. EH19: Bonn 7H **41**
Almond Grn. EH12: Edin 3C **18**
Almond Gro. EH30: S Q'fry 2H **7**
Almondhill Cotts. EH29: Kltn 1C **16**
Almondhill Rd. EH29: Kltn 1B **16**
Almondhill Steading EH29: Kltn 1B **16**
Almond Rd. EH12: Edin A 4E **16**
Almondside EH29: Kltn 2B **16**
Almond Sq. EH12: Edin 3C **18**
Alnwickhill Ct. EH16: Edin 6K **33**
Alnwickhill Cres. EH16: Edin 6K **33**
Alnwickhill Dr. EH16: Edin 6K **33**
Alnwickhill Gdns. EH16: Edin 6K **33**
Alnwickhill Gro. EH16: Edin 6K **33**
Alnwickhill Loan EH16: Edin 6K **33**
Alnwickhill Pk. EH16: Edin 6A **34**
Alnwickhill Rd. EH16: Edin 5A **34**
Alnwickhill Ter. EH16: Edin 6K **33**
Alnwickhill Vw. EH16: Edin 6K **33**
Alvanley Ter. EH9: Edin 6F **21**
Alva Pl. EH7: Edin 2A **22** (1K **5**)
Alva St. EH3: Edin 3E **20** (4A **4**)
Ambassador Ct. EH21: Muss 2F **25**
Amos Path EH20: Loan 6J **39**
Anchor Cl. EH1: Edin 4F **5**
Anchorfield EH6: Newh 4C **12** (not continuous)
Ancrum Bank EH22: Dalk 4B **42**
Ancrum Rd. EH22: Dalk 4B **42**
Anderson Av. EH22: Newt 7D **42**
Anderson Pl. EH6: Edin 5D **12**
Anderson's Cl. EH1: Edin 5E **4**
Andrew Ct. EH26: Pen 7C **44**
Andrew Dodds Av. EH22: May 6F **43**
Andrew Wood Ct. EH6: Newh 4B **12**
Angle Pk. Ter. EH11: Edin 6D **20**
Angres Ct. EH22: Dan 4J **35**
Annandale St. EH7: Edin 7C **12**
Annandale St. La. EH7: Edin 1J **21**
Anne St. EH26: Pen 7C **44**
Annfield EH6: Newh 4C **12**
EH33: Tran 3J **27**
Annfield St. EH6: Newh 4C **12**
Ann St. EH4: Edin 2E **20**
Ann Ter. EH8: Edin 2A **22**
Antigua St. EH7: Edin 1G **5**
Appin St. EH14: Edin 1B **32**
Appin Ter. EH14: Edin 7B **20**
Arboretum Av. EH4: Edin 1E **20**
Arboretum Pl. EH3: Edin 7K **11**
Arboretum Rd. EH3: Edin 6K **11**
Arbuthnot Rd. EH20: Loan 6C **40**
Archibald Pl. EH3: Edin 4G **21** (6D **4**)
Arden St. EH9: Edin 6G **21**
Ardmillan Pl. EH11: Edin 6D **20**
Ardmillan Ter. EH11: Edin 6C **20**
Ardmillan Ter. La. EH11: Edin 6D **20**
Ardshiel Av. EH4: Edin 2E **18**
Argyle Cres. EH15: Port 3H **23**
Argyle Pk. Ter. EH9: Edin 6H **21**
Argyle Pl. EH9: Edin 6H **21**
EH19: Bonn 7F **41**
Argyle St. EH6: Newh 4D **12**
Argyll Ter. EH11: Edin 4E **20**
Armine Pl. EH26: Pen 7F **45**
ARNISTON ENGINE 5D **48**
Arniston Ho. EH4: Edin 7J **11**
Arniston Pl. EH19: Bonn 6H **41**
Arnott Gdns. EH14: Edin 3J **31**
Arnprior Rd. EH23: Gore 6F **49**
Arran Pl. EH15: Port 3J **23**
Arras Gro. EH26: Pen 6D **44**
Arrol Pl. EH30: S Q'fry 2H **7**
Arthur's Seat 5A **22**
Arthur St. EH6: Edin 7E **12**
Arthur St. La. EH6: Edin 7D **12**
Arthur Vw. Cres. EH22: Dan 4H **35**
Arthur Vw. Ter. EH22: Dan 4H **35**
Ashburnham Gdns. EH30: S Q'fry 1J **7**
Ashburnham Loan EH30: S Q'fry 1J **7**
Ashburnham Rd. EH30: S Q'fry 2J **7**
Ash Gro. EH22: May 6G **43**
Ashgrove EH21: Muss 2G **25**
Ashgrove Pl. EH21: Muss 2H **25**
Ashgrove Vw. EH21: Muss 2G **25**
Ash La. EH20: Loan 6J **39**
Ashley Dr. EH11: Edin 1C **32**
Ashley Gdns. EH11: Edin 1C **32**
Ashley Gro. EH11: Edin 7C **20**
Ashley Pl. EH6: Edin 6D **12**
Ashley Ter. EH11: Edin 7C **20**
Ashton Gro. EH16: Edin 3B **34**
Ashton Vs. EH15: Port 4J **23**
Ashville Ter. EH6: Edin 7G **13**
Assembly Rooms 2D **4**
Assembly St. EH6: Leith 5F **13**
Assynt Bank EH26: Pen 1E **50**
ASTLEY AINSLIE HOSPITAL 1G **33**
Atheling Gro. EH30: S Q'fry 2H **7**
Atholl Cres. EH3: Edin 4E **20** (5A **4**)
Atholl Cres. La. EH3: Edin 4E **20** (5A **4**)
Atholl Pl. EH3: Edin 4E **20**
Atholl Ter. EH11: Edin 4E **20**
Attlee Cres. EH22: May 1G **49**
AUCHENDINNY 6G **45**
Auchingane EH10: Edin 7C **32**
Auchinleck Ct. EH6: Newh 4B **12**
Auldgate EH29: Kltn 2B **16**
Auld Orchard EH19: Bonn 6J **41**
Avenue, The EH14: Cur 5B **30**
EH23: Gore 5D **48**
Avenue Rd. EH22: Dalk 3A **42**
EH32: Cock 4G **15**
Avenue Vs. EH4: Edin 1D **20**
Avondale Pl. EH3: Edin 7A **12**
Avon Gro. EH4: Cram 6H **9**
EH26: Pen 1E **50**
Avon Pl. EH4: Cram 6H **9**
Avon Rd. EH4: Cram 6H **9**
Ayres Wynd EH32: Pres 6D **14**

B

Baberton Av. EH14: J Grn 6F **31**
Baberton Cres. EH14: J Grn 6F **31**
BABERTON JUNC. 5G **31**
Baberton Loan EH14: J Grn 6F **31**
Baberton Mains Av. EH14: Edin 5F **31**
Baberton Mains Bank EH14: Edin 5F **31**
Baberton Mains Brae EH14: Edin 5E **30**
Baberton Mains Ct. EH14: Edin 5F **31**
Baberton Mains Cres. EH14: Edin 5F **31**
Baberton Mains Dell EH14: Edin 5E **30**
Baberton Mains Dr. EH14: Edin 5E **30**
Baberton Mains Farm EH14: Edin 4D **30**
Baberton Mains Gdns. EH14: Edin 4E **30**
Baberton Mains Grn. EH14: Edin 5F **31**
Baberton Mains Gro. EH14: Edin 5F **31**
Baberton Mains Hill EH14: Edin 5E **30**
Baberton Mains Lea EH14: Edin 5E **30**
Baberton Mains Loan EH14: Edin 5G **31**
Baberton Mains Pk. EH14: Edin 5F **31**
Baberton Mains Pl. EH14: Edin 5F **31**
Baberton Mains Ri. EH14: Edin 5E **30**
Baberton Mains Row EH14: Edin 5F **31**
Baberton Mains Ter. EH14: Edin 5F **31**
Baberton Mains Vw. EH14: Edin 5F **31**
Baberton Mains Way EH14: Edin 5E **30**
Baberton Mains Wood EH14: Edin 5E **30**
Baberton Mains Wynd EH14: Edin 5F **31**
Baberton Pk. EH14: J Grn 6F **31**
Baberton Sq. EH14: J Grn 6F **31**
Back Dean EH4: Edin 3D **20**
Backdean Rd. EH22: Dan 4G **35**
Backlee EH16: Edin 6A **34** (not continuous)
Back Sta. Rd. EH16: Edin 7D **22**
Baileyfield Cres. EH15: Port 3G **23**
Baileyfield Est. EH15: Port 3G **23**
Baileyfield Rd. EH15: Port 2G **23** (Fishwives' Causeway)
EH15: Port 3G **23** (Sir Harry Lauder Rd.)
Bailie Fife's Cl. EH1: Edin 4G **5**
Bailie Gro. EH15: Port 5H **23**
Bailie Path EH15: Port 5G **23**
Bailie Pl. EH15: Port 5H **23**
Bailie Ter. EH15: Port 5G **23**
Bainfield Bowling and Social Club 7A **20**
Baird Av. EH12: Edin 5A **20**
Baird Dr. EH12: Edin 6K **19**
Baird Gdns. EH12: Edin 5A **20**
Baird Gro. EH12: Edin 5A **20**
Baird Rd. EH28: Rat 7C **16**
Baird's Way EH19: Bonn 7K **41** (not continuous)
Baird Ter. EH12: Edin 5A **20**
Bakehouse Cl. EH8: Edin 4H **5**
Baker's Pl. EH3: Edin 1A **4**
Balbirnie Pl. EH12: Edin 4C **20**
Balcarres Ct. EH10: Edin 2E **32**
Balcarres Pl. EH21: Muss 1F **25**
Balcarres Rd. EH21: Muss 1F **25**
Balcarres St. EH10: Edin 2D **32**
Balderston Gdns. EH16: Edin 3B **34**
Baldwin Ct. EH26: Pen 3C **50**
BALERNO 4E **36**
Balfour Ct. EH12: Edin 2D **18**
Balfour Pl. EH6: Edin 7D **12**
Balfour Sq. EH33: Tran 2H **27** (not continuous)
Balfour St. EH6: Edin 6E **12**
Balfour Ter. EH26: Pen 5F **45**
Balfron Loan EH4: Edin 2E **18**
Balgreen Av. EH12: Edin 5J **19**
Balgreen Gdns. EH12: Edin 5J **19**
Balgreen Pk. EH12: Edin 5K **19**
Balgreen Rd. EH11: Edin 5K **19**
EH12: Edin 5K **19**
Ballantyne La. EH6: Edin 5E **12**
Ballantyne Rd. EH6: Edin 5D **12**
Balmoral Pl. EH3: Edin 7A **12**
Balm Well Av. EH16: Edin 7B **34**
Balm Well Gro. EH16: Edin 7B **34**
Balm Well Pk. EH16: Edin 7B **34**
Balm Well Ter. EH16: Edin 7A **34**
Baltic St. EH6: Leith 5F **13**
BANGHOLM 5A **12**
Bangholm Av. EH5: Edin 5A **12**
Bangholm Bower Av. EH5: Edin 5A **12**
Bangholm Gro. EH5: Edin 5B **12**
Bangholm Loan EH5: Edin 5B **12**
Bangholm Pk. EH5: Edin 5A **12**
Bangholm Pl. EH5: Edin 5A **12**
Bangholm Rd. EH5: Edin 5A **12**
Bangholm Ter. EH3: Edin 6A **12**
Bangholm Vw. EH5: Edin 5B **12**
Bangholm Vs. *EH5: Edin 5B 12 (off Ferry Rd.)*
Bangor Rd. EH6: Edin 5D **12**
Bankfoot EH32: Pres 6B **14**
Bankhead Av. EH11: Edin 1E **30**
Bankhead B'way. EH11: Edin 1D **30**
Bankhead Cotts. EH30: Dalm 2K **7**
Bankhead Crossway Nth. EH11: Edin 1D **30**
Bankhead Crossway Sth. EH11: Edin 2D **30**
Bankhead Dr. EH11: Edin 1D **30**
Bankhead Gro. EH30: Dalm 1J **7**
Bankhead Ind. Est. EH11: Edin 1E **30**
Bankhead Medway EH11: Edin 1E **30**
Bankhead Pl. EH11: Edin 1E **30**
Bankhead Rd. EH30: Dalm 1K **7**
Bankhead Rdbt. EH11: Edin 2E **30**
Bankhead St. EH11: Edin 2D **30**
Bankhead Ter. EH11: Edin 2D **30**
Bankhead Way EH11: Edin 2D **30**
Bankmill *EH26: Pen 3D 50 (off Bridge St.)*
Bankmill Vw. EH26: Pen 3D **50** (not continuous)
Bank of Scotland Mus. 4E **4**
Bankpark Brae EH33: Tran 1F **27**
Bankpark Cres. EH33: Tran 1F **27**
Bankpark Gro. EH33: Tran 1F **27**
Bank St. EH1: Edin 3H **21** (4E **4**)
EH26: Pen 3D **50**
Bankton Ct. EH33: Tran 2H **27**
BANKTON INTERCHANGE 7H **15**
Bankton Ter. EH32: Pres 7F **15**
Barclay Pl. EH10: Edin 5F **21**
Barclay Ter. EH10: Edin 6F **21**
Barleyknowe Cres. EH23: Gore 5E **48**
Barleyknowe Gdns. EH23: Gore 4E **48**
Barleyknowe La. EH23: Gore 5E **48**
Barleyknowe Pl. EH23: Gore 4E **48**
Barleyknowe Rd. EH23: Gore 4E **48**
Barleyknowe St. EH23: Gore 4E **48**
Barleyknowe Ter. EH23: Gore 5E **48**
Barnbougle Ride EH30: S Q'fry 3D **8**
Barn Pk. EH14: Edin 4G **31**
Barn Pk. Cres. EH14: Edin 4G **31**
Barnshot Rd. EH13: Edin 6K **31**
Barntalloch Ct. *EH12: Edin 4D 18 (off Craigievar Wynd)*
BARNTON 7J **9**
Barnton Av. EH4: Edin 6K **9**
Barnton Av. W. EH4: Cram 6J **9**
Barnton Brae EH4: Cram 6J **9**
Barnton Ct. EH4: Edin 7J **9**
Barnton Gdns. EH4: Edin 6B **10**
Barntongate Av. EH4: Edin 1D **18**
Barntongate Dr. EH4: Edin 1D **18**
Barntongate Ter. EH4: Edin 1D **18**
Barnton Gro. EH4: Cram, Edin 7J **9**
BARNTON JUNCTION 1D **18**
Barnton Loan EH4: Edin 6B **10**
Barnton Pk. EH4: Edin 6B **10**
Barnton Pk. Av. EH4: Edin 7K **9**
Barnton Pk. Cres. EH4: Edin 7J **9**
Barnton Pk. Dell EH4: Edin 7A **10**
Barnton Pk. Dr. EH4: Edin 7K **9**
Barnton Pk. Gdns. EH4: Edin 7K **9**
Barnton Pk. Gro. EH4: Edin 7K **9**
Barnton Pk. Pl. EH4: Edin 7A **10**
Barnton Pk. Vw. EH4: Edin 7J **9**
Barnton Pk. Wood EH4: Edin 1D **18**
Barondale Cotts. EH22: Dalk 5C **42**
Baron Maule's Cl. EH1: Edin 4G **5**
Baronscourt Rd. EH8: Edin 2C **22**
Baronscourt Ter. EH8: Edin 2D **22**
Barony Pl. EH3: Edin 1H **21** (1E **4**)
Barony St. EH3: Edin 1H **21** (1E **4**)
Barony Ter. EH12: Edin 4F **19**
Barrace Steps EH1: Edin 5C **4**
Barracks St. EH32: Port S 3H **15**
Bathfield EH6: Newh 4D **12**
Bath Pl. EH15: Port 2H **23**
Bath Rd. EH6: Leith 5G **13**
Bath St. EH15: Port 3H **23**
Bath St. La. EH15: Port 3H **23**
Bavelaw Cres. EH26: Pen 1B **50**

Broomhall Pk.—Canaan La.

Broomhall Pk. EH12: Edin 6F **19**
Broomhall Pl. EH12: Edin 6F **19**
Broomhall Rd. EH12: Edin 6E **18**
Broomhall Ter. EH12: Edin 6F **19**
Broomhill Av. EH26: Pen 3C **50**
Broomhill Dr. EH22: Dalk 4A **42**
Broomhill Pk. EH22: Dalk 4A **42**
Broomhill Rd. EH26: Pen 3C **50**
BROOMHOUSE 1G 31
Broomhouse Av. EH11: Edin 1F **31**
Broomhouse Bank
EH11: Edin 1G **31**
Broomhouse Cotts.
EH11: Edin 1F **31**
Broomhouse Cotts. E.
EH11: Edin 1G **31**
Broomhouse Cotts. W.
EH11: Edin 1F **31**
Broomhouse Ct. EH11: Edin 1G **31**
Broomhouse Cres.
EH11: Edin 1G **31**
Broomhouse Dr. EH11: Edin 7F **19**
Broomhouse Gdns.
EH11: Edin 7F **19**
Broomhouse Gdns. E.
EH11: Edin 7G **19**
Broomhouse Gdns. W.
EH11: Edin 7F **19**
Broomhouse Gro. EH11: Edin ...1G **31**
Broomhouse Loan EH11: Edin ...1G **31**
Broomhouse Mkt. *EH11: Edin ...1G **31***
(off Broomhouse Pl. N.)
Broomhouse Medway
EH11: Edin 7G **19**
Broomhouse Pk. EH11: Edin 1F **31**
Broomhouse Path *EH11: Edin ...1F **31***
(off Broomhouse Av.)
Broomhouse Pl. Nth.
EH11: Edin 1F **31**
Broomhouse Pl. Sth.
EH11: Edin 1G **31**
Broomhouse Rd. EH11: Edin 7F **19**
EH12: Edin 7F **19**
Broomhouse Row EH11: Edin ...7G **19**
Broomhouse Sq. EH11: Edin 1G **31**
Broomhouse St. Nth.
EH11: Edin 1F **31**
Broomhouse St. Sth.
EH11: Edin 2G **31**
Broomhouse Ter. EH11: Edin ...7G **19**
Broomhouse Wlk. EH11: Edin ...1G **31**
Broomhouse Way EH11: Edin ...1G **31**
Broomhouse Wynd
*EH11: Edin 1G **31***
(off Broomhouse Ct.)
Broomieknowe EH18: Las 5G **41**
Broomieknowe Gdns.
EH19: Bonn 5H **41**
Broomieknowe Pk.
EH19: Bonn 5H **41**
Broomlea Cres. EH12: Edin 6F **19**
Broompark Bus. Pk.
*EH5: Edin 3H **11***
(off New Broompark)
Broompark Rd. EH12: Edin 6F **19**
Broomside Ter. EH12: Edin 6G **19**
Broomview Ho. EH11: Edin 2F **31**
Broomyknowe EH14: Edin 4K **31**
Brougham Pl.
EH3: Edin 5G **21** (7C **4**)
Brougham St.
EH3: Edin 5F **21** (7B **4**)
BROUGHTON 1H 21
Broughton Mkt.
EH3: Edin 2H **21** (1E **4**)
Broughton Pl.
EH1: Edin 1H **21** (1F **5**)
Broughton Pl. La. EH1: Edin 1H **21**
Broughton Rd. EH7: Edin 7C **12**
Broughton St.
EH1: Edin 1H **21** (1F **5**)
Broughton St. La.
EH1: Edin 2H **21** (1F **5**)
Brown's Cl. EH8: Edin 3K **21** (3J **5**)
Brown's Ct. EH8: Edin 3J **5**
Brown's Pl. EH1: Edin 5D **4**
Brown St. EH8: Edin 4J **21** (6H **5**)
Brown St. La. EH8: Edin 6H **5**
Bruce Gdns. EH22: Dalk 3D **42**
Bruce St. EH10: Edin 2E **32**
BRUNSTANE 5K 23
Brunstane Bank EH15: Port 5K **23**
Brunstane Cres. EH15: Port 5K **23**
Brunstane Dr. EH15: Port 5J **23**
Brunstane Gdns. EH15: Port 4J **23**
EH26: Pen 1B **50**
Brunstane Gdns. M.
EH15: Port 4J **23**
Brunstane Mill Rd.
EH15: Port 1B **24**
Brunstane Rd. EH15: Port 4J **23**
Brunstane Rd. Nth.
EH15: Port 3J **23**
Brunstane Rd. Sth.
EH15: Edin, Port 5J **23**
Brunstane Station (Rail) 5J **23**
Brunswick Rd. EH7: Edin 1J **21**
Brunswick St.
EH7: Edin 1J **21** (1H **5**)
Brunswick St. La.
EH7: Edin 1J **21** (1H **5**)
Brunswick Ter. EH7: Edin 1K **21**
Brunton Ct. EH21: Muss 2E **24**
Brunton Gdns.
EH7: Edin 1K **21** (1K **5**)
Brunton Pl. EH7: Edin 1K **21** (1J **5**)
Brunton's Cl. EH22: Dalk 2C **42**
Brunton Ter. EH7: Edin ...1K **21** (1K **5**)
Brunton Theatre 2E **24**
BRUNTSFIELD 6G 21
Bruntsfield Av. EH10: Edin 6F **21**
Bruntsfield Cres. EH10: Edin 6F **21**
Bruntsfield Gdns. EH10: Edin 7F **21**
Bruntsfield Pl. EH10: Edin 6F **21**
Bruntsfield Ter. EH10: Edin 6F **21**
BRYANS 7D 42
Bryans Av. EH22: Newt 7D **42**
Bryans Rd. EH22: Newt 7C **42**
Bryce Av. EH7: Edin 1F **23**
Bryce Cres. EH14: Cur 7C **30**
Bryce Gdns. EH14: Cur 7C **30**
Bryce Gro. EH7: Edin 1F **23**
Bryce Pl. EH14: Cur 7C **30**
Bryce Rd. EH14: Cur 7C **30**
Bryson Rd. EH11: Edin 6D **20**
Buccleuch Ct. EH22: Dalk 1B **42**
Buccleuch Pend EH8: Edin 7G **5**
Buccleuch Pl.
EH8: Edin 5H **21** (7F **5**)
Buccleuch St.
EH8: Edin 5J **21** (7G **5**)
EH22: Dalk 2C **42**
Buccleuch Ter.
EH8: Edin 5J **21** (7G **5**)
Buccleugh Pl. La. EH8: Edin 7G **5**
Buchanan St. EH7: Edin 7E **12**
Buckie Rd. EH22: May 7G **43**
Buckingham Ter. EH4: Edin 2D **20**
Buckstane Pk. EH10: Edin 5E **32**
Buckstone Av. EH10: Edin 6F **33**
Buckstone Bank EH10: Edin 5F **33**
Buckstone Circ. EH10: Edin 6G **33**
Buckstone Cl. EH10: Edin 6G **33**
Buckstone Ct. EH10: Edin 6F **33**
Buckstone Cres. EH10: Edin 5F **33**
Buckstone Crook EH10: Edin 7G **33**
Buckstone Dell EH10: Edin 5F **33**
Buckstone Dr. EH10: Edin 5F **33**
Buckstone Gdns. EH10: Edin 6F **33**
Buckstone Ga. EH10: Edin 6G **33**
Buckstone Grn. EH10: Edin 6G **33**
Buckstone Gro. EH10: Edin 5F **33**
Buckstone Hill EH10: Edin 5F **33**
Buckstone Howe EH10: Edin 6G **33**
Buckstone Lea EH10: Edin 6G **33**
Buckstone Loan EH10: Edin 6F **33**
Buckstone Loan E.
EH10: Edin 6G **33**
Buckstone Neuk EH10: Edin 5G **33**
Buckstone Pl. EH10: Edin 6F **33**
Buckstone Ri. EH10: Edin 6G **33**
Buckstone Rd. EH10: Edin 6F **33**
Buckstone Row EH10: Edin 5G **33**
Buckstone Shaw EH10: Edin 7G **33**
Buckstone Ter. EH10: Edin 6F **33**
(not continuous)
Buckstone Vw. EH10: Edin 5F **33**
Buckstone Way EH10: Edin 5F **33**
Buckstone Wood EH10: Edin 6F **33**
Buckstone Wynd EH10: Edin 6G **33**
BUGHTLIN 3D 18
Bughtlin Dr. EH12: Edin 2C **18**
Bughtlin Gdns. EH12: Edin 3C **18**
Bughtlin Grn. EH12: Edin 2C **18**
Bughtlin Loan EH12: Edin 3C **18**
Bughtlin Mkt. EH12: Edin 3D **18**
Bughtlin Pk. EH12: Edin 3D **18**
Bughtlin Pl. EH12: Edin 2C **18**
Builyeon Rd. EH30: S Q'fry 2E **6**
Bull's Cl. EH8: Edin 3K **21** (3J **5**)
BURDIEHOUSE 1B 40
Burdiehouse Av. EH17: Edin 1B **40**
Burdiehouse Cres.
EH17: Edin 1B **40**
Burdiehouse Crossway
EH17: Edin 1B **40**
Burdiehouse Dr. EH17: Edin 1B **40**
Burdiehouse Loan EH17: Edin ...1B **40**
Burdiehouse Medway
EH17: Edin 1B **40**
Burdiehouse Pl. EH17: Edin 1B **40**
Burdiehouse Rd. EH17: Edin 7A **34**
Burdiehouse Sq. EH17: Edin 2A **40**
Burdiehouse St. EH17: Edin 1B **40**
Burdiehouse Ter. EH17: Edin ...1B **40**
Burgess Rd. EH30: S Q'fry 1H **7**
Burgess St. EH6: Leith 5F **13**
Burgess Ter. EH9: Edin 7A **22**
Burghlee Cres. EH20: Loan 6B **40**
Burghlee Ter. EH20: Loan 6B **40**
Burghtoft EH17: Edin 7E **34**
Burlington St. EH6: Edin 5E **12**
Burnbank EH20: Loan 5A **40**
Burnbank Cotts. EH28: Nbdge ...5B **16**
Burnbank Cres. EH20: Loan 4A **40**
Burnbank Gro. EH20: Loan 4A **40**
Burnbank Ter. EH25: Bil 7J **39**
Burnbrae EH12: Edin 3C **18**
Burndene Dr. EH20: Loan 4K **39**
Burnet's Cl. EH1: Edin 4F **5**
Burnhead Cres. EH16: Edin 5A **34**
Burnhead Gro. EH16: Edin 6B **34**
Burnhead Loan EH16: Edin 6B **34**
Burnhead Path E. EH16: Edin ...6B **34**
Burnhead Path W. EH16: Edin ...6A **34**
BURNSHOT JUNC. 5F 9
Burnside EH11: Edin 1J **31**
EH12: Edin 3C **18**
EH32: Pres 6C **14**
Burnside Av. EH22: East 6F **43**
Burnside Cres. EH22: East 6F **43**
Burnside Pk. EH14: Bal 4E **36**
Burnside Rd. EH12: Edin A 3G **17**
EH23: Gore 5E **48**
Burns Monument 2J **5**
Burns Pl. *EH6: Edin 6C **12***
(off Newhaven Rd.)
Burns St. EH6: Edin 6F **13**
Bush Est., The EH26: Pen 3F **45**
BUSH LOAN 2G 45
Bush St. EH21: Muss 2D **24**
Bush Ter. EH21: Muss 2D **24**
Butlerfield Ind. Est.
EH19: Bonn 2C **48**
Butts, The *EH33: Tran 2G **27***
(off Market Vw.)
Buxley Rd. EH33: Elph 7F **27**
Byer's Cl. EH1: Edin 4E **4**

C

Cables Wynd EH6: Leith 5E **12**
Cables Wynd Ho. EH6: Leith 5E **12**
Caddells Row EH4: Cram 5J **9**
Cadell Pl. EH32: Cock 3G **15**
Cadell Sq. EH33: Tran 2H **27**
Cadiz St. EH6: Leith 5F **13**
Cadogan Rd. EH16: Edin 5A **34**
Cadzow Pl. EH7: Edin 2A **22**
Caerketton Av. EH25: Bil 7J **39**
Caerketton Cotts.
EH13: Edin 4C **32**
Caerketton Ct. EH13: Edin 5D **32**
Caerlaverock Ct. *EH12: Edin 4D **18***
(off Craigievar Wynd)
Caesar Rd. EH33: Tran 2G **27**
Caesar Way EH33: Tran 2G **27**
Cairds Row EH21: Muss 1D **24**
Cairnbank Gdns. EH26: Pen 3C **50**
Cairnbank Rd. EH26: Pen 3C **50**
Cairnmuir Rd. EH12: Edin 3G **19**
Cairns Dr. EH14: Bal 5D **36**
Cairns Gdns. EH14: Bal 5D **36**
Cairntows Cl. EH16: Edin 7D **22**
Caithness Pl. EH5: Edin 5A **12**
Caiyside EH10: Edin 7E **32**
Caiystane Av. EH10: Edin 7E **32**
Caiystane Cres. EH10: Edin 6E **32**
Caiystane Dr. EH10: Edin 7D **32**
Caiystane Gdns. EH10: Edin 6D **32**
Caiystane Hill EH10: Edin 6E **32**
Caiystane Ter. EH10: Edin 7D **32**
Caiystane Vw. EH10: Edin 7E **32**
Calder Ct. EH11: Edin 2E **30**
Calder Cres. EH11: Edin 3D **30**
Calder Dr. EH11: Edin 3E **30**
Calder Gdns. EH11: Edin 3D **30**
Calder Gro. EH11: Edin 3D **30**
CALDER JUNC. 3D 30
Calder Pk. EH11: Edin 3E **30**
Calder Pl. EH11: Edin 3E **30**
Calder Rd. EH11: Edin 2D **30**
(not continuous)
EH14: Cur 3B **30**
Calder Rd. Gdns. EH11: Edin ...1J **31**
Calder Vw. EH11: Edin 3D **30**
Caledonia Ho. EH12: Edin 7C **18**
Caledonian Cres.
EH11: Edin 5D **20**
Caledonian Pl. EH11: Edin 5D **20**
Caledonian Rd. EH11: Edin 5E **20**
CALTON 2K 21 (1K 5)
Calton Hill 2J **21** (2G **5**)
Calton Hill EH1: Edin 2J **21** (2F **5**)
Calton Hill Stairs EH8: Edin 3H **5**
Calton Rd. EH1: Edin 2H **21** (2F **5**)
EH7: Edin 3H **21** (3F **5**)
EH8: Edin 3J **21** (3H **5**)
Cambridge Av. EH6: Edin 7D **12**
Cambridge Gdns. EH6: Edin 7D **12**
Cambridge St.
EH1: Edin 4F **21** (5B **4**)
Cambusnethan St. EH7: Edin ...2B **22**
Cameo Cinema 5F **21** (7B **4**)
Camera Obscura & Outlook Tower
..............4D **4**
Cameron Cres. EH16: Edin 1B **34**
EH19: Bonn 1E **46**
Cameron Ho. Av. EH16: Edin ...7B **22**
Cameron March EH16: Edin 1A **34**
Cameron Pk. EH16: Edin 1B **34**
Cameron Smail Rd.
EH14: Cur 5A **30**
Cameron Ter. EH16: Edin 1B **34**
Cameron Toll Gdns.
EH16: Edin 1B **34**
CAMERON TOLL RDBT. 1B 34
Cameron Toll Shop. Cen.
EH16: Edin 1A **34**
CAMMO 1B 18
Cammo Bank EH4: Cram 1C **18**
Cammo Brae EH4: Cram 1C **18**
Cammo Cres. EH4: Cram 1C **18**
Cammo Gdns. EH4: Cram 1C **18**
Cammo Gro. EH4: Cram 1B **18**
Cammo Hill EH4: Cram 1B **18**
Cammo Parkway EH4: Cram 1C **18**
Cammo Pl. EH4: Cram 1C **18**
Cammo Rd. EH4: Cram, Edin 1A **18**
EH12: Edin 2J **17**
Cammo Wlk.
EH4: Cram, Edin 1B **18**
Campbell Av. EH12: Edin 4A **20**
Campbell Pk. Cres.
EH13: Edin 6H **31**
Campbell Pk. Dr. EH13: Edin ...6H **31**
Campbell Rd. EH12: Edin 3A **20**
Campbell's Cl.
EH8: Edin 3K **21** (3J **5**)
Campie Ct. EH21: Muss 2D **24**
Campie Gdns. EH21: Muss 2D **24**
(not continuous)
Campie La. EH21: Muss 2D **24**
Campie Rd. EH21: Muss 3D **24**
Camp Rd. EH22: May 6G **43**
Campview EH22: Dan 5H **35**
Campview Av. EH22: Dan 5H **35**
Campview Cres. EH22: Dan 5H **35**
Campview Gdns. EH22: Dan 5H **35**
Campview Gro. EH22: Dan 5J **35**
Campview Rd. EH19: Bonn 6H **41**
Campview Ter. EH22: Dan 5H **35**
Camp Wood Vw. EH22: May 1G **49**
Camus Av. EH10: Edin 6E **32**
Camus Pk. EH10: Edin 6E **32**
Canaan La. EH9: Edin 1F **33**
EH10: Edin 1G **33**

Candlemaker Row
EH1: Edin 4H **21** (5E **4**)
Candlemaker's Cres.
EH17: Edin 6F **35**
Candlemaker's Pk.
EH17: Edin 6F **35**
Canmore St. EH30: S Q'fry 2G **7**
Canning St. EH3: Edin 4F **21** (4A **4**)
Canning St. La. EH3: Edin 5A **4**
Cannon Wynd EH6: Newh 4D **12**
CANONGATE . . . .**3J 21 (3H 5)**
Canongate EH8: Edin 3J **21** (4G **5**)
Canongate Kirk 3H 5
Canongate Tolbooth
EH8: Edin 3H 5
Canon La. EH3: Edin 1G **21**
CANONMILLS **7B 12**
Canonmills EH3: Edin 7B **12**
Canonmills Bri. *EH3: Edin 7B* ***12***
(off Huntly St.)
Canon St. EH3: Edin 7B **12**
Capelaw Ct. EH13: Edin 5C **32**
Capelaw Rd. EH13: Edin 7J **31**
Caplaw Way EH26: Pen 2A **50**
Caponhall Ct. EH33: Tran 3G **27**
Caponhall Dr. EH33: Tran 3G **27**
Caponhall Rd. EH33: Tran 3G **27**
Caponhall Way EH33: Tran 2G **27**
Captain's Dr. EH16: Edin 6A **34**
Captain's Loan EH16: Edin 6B **34**
Captain's Rd. EH17: Edin 7A **34**
Captain's Row EH16: Edin 7B **34**
Carberry Cl. EH21: Muss 5F **25**
Carberry Ct. EH21: Whit 7G **25**
Carberry Gro. EH21: Muss 5F **25**
Carberry Pl. EH12: Edin 4C **20**
Carberry Rd. EH21: Muss 4F **25**
Carfrae Gdns. EH4: Edin 1J **19**
Carfrae Gro. EH4: Edin 1J **19**
Carfrae Pk. EH4: Edin 1J **19**
Carfrae Rd. EH4: Edin 1J **19**
Cargil Ct. EH5: Edin 5A **12**
Cargilfield Vw. EH4: Cram 6J **9**
Cargil Ter. EH5: Edin 5K **11**
Carlaverock Av. EH33: Tran 3H **27**
Carlaverock Cl. EH33: Tran 4J **27**
Carlaverock Ct. EH33: Tran 3J **27**
Carlaverock Cres.
EH33: Tran 3H **27**
Carlaverock Dr. EH33: Tran 3H **27**
Carlaverock Gro. EH33: Tran . . .3H **27**
Carlaverock Ter. EH33: Tran 4J **27**
Carlaverock Vw. EH33: Tran 4H **27**
Carlaverock Wlk. EH33: Tran . . .3H **27**
Carlops Av. EH26: Pen 1C **50**
Carlops Cres. EH26: Pen 1C **50**
Carlops Rd. EH26: Pen 2A **50**
Carlowrie Av. EH30: Dalm 3K **7**
Carlowrie Cres. EH30: Dalm 3K **7**
Carlowrie Pl. EH23: Gore 5F **49**
Carlton St. EH4: Edin 2E **20** (1A **4**)
Carlton Ter. EH7: Edin 2K **21** (1J **5**)
Carlton Ter. Brae
EH7: Edin 2K **21** (1K **5**)
Carlton Ter. La.
EH7: Edin 2K **21** (1J **5**)
Carlton Ter. M.
EH7: Edin 2K **21** (1J **5**)
Carlyle Pl. EH7: Edin 2A **22**
EH21: Muss 2E **24**
Carmel Av. EH29: Kltn 1A **16**
Carmelite Rd. EH30: S Q'fry 2G **7**
Carmel Rd. EH29: Kltn 2A **16**
Carnbee Av. EH16: Edin 6C **34**
Carnbee Cres. EH16: Edin 6C **34**
Carnbee Dell EH16: Edin 6C **34**
Carnbee End EH16: Edin 6C **34**
Carnbee Pk. EH16: Edin 6C **34**
Carnegie Ct. EH8: Edin 6H **5**
Carnegie St. EH8: Edin . . .4J **21** (6H **5**)
Carnethie St. EH24: Rose 6D **46**
Carnethy Av. EH13: Edin 6J **31**
EH26: Pen 1C **50**
Carnethy Ct. EH26: Pen 2D **50**
Caroline Gdns. EH12: Edin 4G **19**
Caroline Pk. Av. EH5: Edin 3G **11**
Caroline Pk. Gro. EH5: Edin 4G **11**
Caroline Pl. EH12: Edin 4G **19**
Caroline Ter. EH12: Edin 3E **18**
Carpet La. EH6: Leith 5F **13**
Carrick Cres. EH22: East 5E **42**
CARRICK KNOWE **6H 19**
Carrick Knowe Av.
EH12: Edin 5H **19**
Carrick Knowe Dr.
EH12: Edin 6H **19**
Carrick Knowe Gdns.
EH12: Edin 6H **19**
Carrick Knowe Gro.
EH12: Edin 6H **19**
Carrick Knowe Hill
EH12: Edin 6H **19**
Carrick Knowe Loan
EH12: Edin 6G **19**
Carrick Knowe Parkway
EH12: Edin 6G **19**
Carrick Knowe Pl. EH12: Edin . . .6H **19**
Carrick Knowe Rd.
EH12: Edin 7G **19**
Carrick Knowe Ter.
EH12: Edin 6H **19**
Carrington Cres. EH4: Edin 7H **11**
Carrington Ho. EH4: Edin 7H **11**
Carrington Rd. EH4: Edin 1C **20**
Carron Pl. EH6: Leith 5G **13**
Carruber's Cl. EH1: Edin 3F **5**
Cars of the Stars Motor Mus. . . .5F 17
Casselbank St. EH6: Edin 6E **12**
Cassel's La. EH6: Edin 6E **12**
Cast, The EH18: Las 7D **40**
Castle Av. EH12: Edin 6F **19**
EH23: Gore 6E **48**
EH32: Port S 3J **15**
Castlebarns Steps EH1: Edin 5B **4**
Castlebrae Bus. Cen.
EH16: Edin 7D **22**
Castlebrae Glebe EH16: Edin . . .7D **22**
Castlebrae Gro. EH16: Edin 1D **34**
Castlebrae Pl. EH16: Edin 1D **34**
Castlebrae Rigg EH16: Edin 1D **34**
Castlehill EH1: Edin 3G **21** (4D **4**)
EH33: Elph 7F ***27***
(off Main St.)
Castlelaw Ct. EH26: Pen 1D **50**
Castlelaw Cres. EH25: Bil 1J **45**
Castlelaw Rd. EH13: Edin 6J **31**
Castlepark Gait EH16: Edin 7D **22**
Castlepark Glade EH16: Edin . . .1D **34**
Castle Pk. Grn. EH16: Edin 7D **22**
Castle Pl. EH23: Gore 6E **48**
Castle Rd. EH32: Port S 3J **15**
EH33: Tran 4F **27**
Castle St. EH2: Edin 3F **21** (3B **4**)
Castle Ter. EH1: Edin 4F **21** (4B **4**)
EH32: Port S 3J **15**
Castle Vw. EH23: Gore 7E **48**
EH32: Port S 3J **15**
Castleview Ho. EH17: Edin 3D **34**
Castle Wlk. EH32: Port S 3J **15**
Castle Wynd Nth. EH1: Edin 5D **4**
Castle Wynd Sth. EH1: Edin 5D **4**
Cathcart Pl. EH11: Edin 5D **20**
Cathedral La.
EH1: Edin 2H **21** (1F **5**)
Catriona Ter. EH26: Pen 5F **45**
Cauldcoats Cotts.
EH22: Dalk 2H **35**
Causeway, The EH15: Edin 5C **22**
Causewayside EH9: Edin 6J **21**
Cavalry Pk. Dr. EH15: Edin 5D **22**
Cedar Dr. EH32: Port S 4G **15**
Cedar Rd. EH20: Loan 6J **39**
Cedars, The EH13: Edin 5K **31**
Cemetery Rd. EH22: Dalk 2B **42**
EH32: Pres 5D **14**
Chalmers Bldgs. EH3: Edin 7A **4**
Chalmer's Cl. EH1: Edin 4G **5**
Chalmers Cres. EH9: Edin 6H **21**
Chalmers St.
EH3: Edin 4G **21** (6D **4**)
Chamberlain Rd. EH10: Edin 7F **21**
Chambers St.
EH1: Edin 4H **21** (5E **4**)
Champigny Ct. EH21: Muss 3G **25**
Chancelot Cres. EH6: Edin 5B **12**
Chancelot Gro. EH5: Edin 5B **12**
Chancelot Ter. EH6: Edin 5B **12**
Chapel Ct. EH16: Edin 7E **22**
Chapel La. *EH6: Leith 5F* ***13***
(off Carpet La.)
Chapel Loan EH25: Rosl 3A **46**
Chapel St. EH8: Edin 4J **21** (6G **5**)
Chap Wynd EH1: Edin 5C **4**
Chariot Dr. EH28: Nbdge 6A **16**
Charlesfield EH8: Edin . . .4H **21** (6F **5**)
Charles St. EH8: Edin 4H **21** (6F **5**)
EH26: Pen 7C **44**
Charles St. La.
EH8: Edin 4H **21** (6F **5**)
Charlotte La.
EH2: Edin 3F **21** (3A **4**)
Charlotte Sq.
EH2: Edin 3F **21** (3A **4**)
Charlton Gro. EH25: Rosl 3K **45**
Charterhall Gro. EH9: Edin 1H **33**
Charterhall Rd. EH9: Edin 2H **33**
Cherry La. EH22: May 7G **43**
Cherry Rd. EH19: Bonn 7H **41**
Cherry Tree Av. EH14: Bal 2G **37**
Cherry Tree Cres.
EH14: Bal, Cur 2F **37**
Cherry Tree Gdns. EH14: Bal 2F **37**
Cherry Tree Gro. EH14: Bal 2F **37**
Cherry Tree Loan EH14: Bal 2G **37**
Cherry Tree Pk. EH14: Bal 2F **37**
Cherry Tree Pl. EH14: Cur 2G **37**
Cherry Tree Vw. EH14: Bal 2G **37**
Chessel's Ct. EH8: Edin . . .3J **21** (4G **5**)
Chesser Av. EH14: Edin 7K **19**
Chesser Cotts. EH11: Edin 7A **20**
Chesser Cres. EH14: Edin 1A **32**
Chesser Gdns. EH14: Edin 7K **19**
Chesser Gro. EH14: Edin 1K **31**
Chesser Loan EH14: Edin 1K **31**
Chester Ct. EH19: Bonn 7G **41**
Chester Dr. EH22: May 1F **49**
Chester Gro. EH19: Bonn 7H **41**
Chester St. EH12: Edin 3E **20**
Chesters Vw. EH19: Bonn 7H **41**
Chester Vw. EH22: May 1F **49**
Chestnut Gro. EH19: Bonn 7H **41**
Chestnut St. EH5: Edin 3H **11**
Cheyne St. EH4: Edin 1E **20**
Childhood Mus. 3J 21 (4G 5)
Chisholm Ter. EH26: Pen 7D **44**
Christian Cres. EH15: Port 4H **23**
Christian Gro. EH15: Port 4H **23**
Christian Path EH15: Port 3G **23**
Christiemiller Av. EH7: Edin 1E **22**
Christiemiller Gro. EH7: Edin . . .2E **22**
Christiemiller Pl. EH7: Edin 2E **22**
Chuckie Pend
EH3: Edin 4F **21** (6A **4**)
Church Hill EH10: Edin 7F **21**
Church Hill Dr. EH10: Edin 7F **21**
Church Hill Pl. EH10: Edin 7F **21**
Church Hill Theatre 7F 21
Church La. EH21: Muss 3E **24**
Church Rd. EH18: Las 4F **41**
Church St. EH20: Loan 6C **40**
EH33: Tran 1G **27**
Cinderhall Pl. EH33: Elph 7F **27**
Circle, The EH22: Dan 4H **35**
Circus Gdns. EH3: Edin . . .2F **21** (1B **4**)
Circus La. EH3: Edin 1F **21** (1B **4**)
Circus Pl. EH3: Edin 2F **21** (1B **4**)
Citadel Pl. EH6: Leith 4E **12**
Citadel St. EH6: Leith 4E **12**
City Art Cen. 3H 21 (3F 5)
City Observatory 2J 21 (2G 5)
City of Edinburgh By-Pass, The
EH10: Edin 7C **32**
EH12: Edin 6B **18**
EH13: Edin 1A **38**
EH14: Edin, J Grn 1B **30**
EH17: Edin 3A **40**
EH18: Las 3A **40**
EH21: Muss 7D **24**
EH22: Dalk, Dan . . .3A **40** & 7D **24**
Civic Sq. EH33: Tran 2H **27**
Clackmae Gro. EH16: Edin 4K **33**
Clackmae Rd. EH16: Edin 4K **33**
Clan Tartan Cen.
Leith Mills 5D 12
Clapper La. EH16: Edin 2A **34**
Clarebank Cres. EH6: Edin 6G **13**
Claremont Bank EH7: Edin 1H **21**
Claremont Ct. EH7: Edin 7C **12**
Claremont Cres. EH7: Edin 7C **12**
Claremont Gdns. EH6: Edin 6G **13**
Claremont Gro. EH7: Edin 7C **12**
Claremont Pk. EH6: Edin 6G **13**
Claremont Rd. EH6: Edin 6G **13**
Clarence St. EH3: Edin 1F **21**
Clarendon Cres. EH4: Edin 2E **20**
Clarinda Gdns. EH22: Dalk 3F **43**
Clarinda Ter. EH16: Edin 4A **34**
Clark Av. EH5: Edin 5B **12**
Clark Gro. EH14: Cur 2G **37**
Clark Pl. EH5: Edin 5A **12**
Clark Rd. EH5: Edin 5A **12**
Claverhouse Dr. EH16: Edin 4A **34**
Clayhills Gro. EH14: Bal 4D **36**
Clayhills Pk. EH14: Bal 4D **36**
CLAYKNOWES **3C 24**
Clayknowes Av. EH21: Muss 3C **24**
Clayknowes Ct. EH21: Muss 4C **24**
Clayknowes Dr. EH21: Muss 3B **24**
Clayknowes Pl. EH21: Muss 3B **24**
Clayknowes Rd. EH21: Muss . . .3C **24**
Clayknowes Way EH21: Muss . . .3C **24**
CLAYLANDS INTERCHANGE **7A 16**
Claylands Rd. EH28: Nbdge 1A **28**
Clearburn Cres. EH16: Edin 7B **22**
Clearburn Gdns. EH16: Edin 7B **22**
Clearburn Rd. EH16: Edin 7B **22**
EH23: Gore 4D **48**
Cleekim Dr. EH15: Edin 7H **23**
Cleekim Rd. EH15: Edin 7H **23**
Cleikiminfield EH15: Edin 7H **23**
Cleikiminrig EH15: Edin 7H **23**
Cleric's Hill EH29: Kltn 2A **16**
Clerk Rd. EH26: Pen 2B **50**
Clerk St. EH8: Edin 5J **21** (7G **5**)
EH20: Loan 5C **40**
CLERMISTON **1F 19**
Clermiston Av. EH4: Edin 1F **19**
Clermiston Cres. EH4: Edin 1F **19**
Clermiston Dr. EH4: Edin 2F **19**
Clermiston Gdns. EH4: Edin 2F **19**
Clermiston Grn. EH4: Edin 1F **19**
Clermiston Gro. EH4: Edin 2F **19**
Clermiston Hill EH4: Edin 1F **19**
Clermiston Junc. EH4: Edin 7A **10**
Clermiston Loan EH4: Edin 1F **19**
Clermiston Medway EH4: Edin . . .1F **19**
Clermiston Pk. EH4: Edin 1F **19**
Clermiston Pl. EH4: Edin 2F **19**
Clermiston Rd. EH12: Edin 4G **19**
Clermiston Rd. Nth.
EH4: Edin 1G **19**
Clermiston Ter. EH12: Edin 4G **19**
Clermiston Vw. EH4: Edin 1G **19**
Clerwood Bank EH12: Edin 3F **19**
Clerwood Gdns. EH12: Edin 3F **19**
Clerwood Gro. EH12: Edin 3G **19**
Clerwood Loan EH12: Edin 3F **19**
Clerwood Pk. EH12: Edin 3F **19**
Clerwood Pl. EH12: Edin 3G **19**
Clerwood Row EH12: Edin 3F **19**
Clerwood Ter. EH12: Edin 3G **19**
Clerwood Vw. EH12: Edin 3G **19**
Clerwood Way EH12: Edin 3F **19**
Cliftonhall Rd. EH28: Nbdge 6A **16**
Clifton Ter. EH12: Edin 4D **20**
Clifton Trad. Est.
EH28: Nbdge 7A **16**
Clinton Rd. EH9: Edin 7F **21**
Clockmill La. EH8: Edin 2B **22**
Clocktower Bus. Pk.
EH12: Edin 7E **18**
Close, The EH30: S Q'fry 2E **6**
Clovenstone Dr. EH14: Edin 5G **31**
Clovenstone Gdns.
EH14: Edin 4G **31**
Clovenstone Pk. EH14: Edin 5G **31**
Clovenstone Rd. EH14: Edin 3G **31**
Clovenstone Rdbt.
EH14: Edin 5G **31**
Cloverfoot Cotts. EH16: Edin 2G **35**
Clufflat EH30: S Q'fry 1E **6**
Cluny Av. EH10: Edin 2F **33**
Cluny Dr. EH10: Edin 2F **33**
Cluny Gdns. EH10: Edin 2F **33**
Cluny Pl. EH10: Edin 1G **33**
Cluny Ter. EH10: Edin 1F **33**
Clyde St. EH2: Edin 2H **21** (2E **4**)
Coalgate Av. EH33: Tran 1J **27**
Coalgate Rd. EH33: Tran 1H **27**
Coalhill EH6: Leith 5E **12**
Coal Neuk EH33: Tran 2G **27**
Coal Neuk Ct. EH33: Tran 2G **27**
COATES **3D 20**
Coates Cres. EH3: Edin . . .4E **20** (4A **4**)
Coates Gdns. EH12: Edin 4D **20**
Coates Pl. EH12: Edin 4E **20**
Coatfield La. EH6: Leith 5F **13**
Cobbinshaw Ho. EH11: Edin 3E **30**

Cobden Cres. EH9: Edin 7K 21
Cobden Rd. EH9: Edin 7K 21
Cobden Ter. EH11: Edin 4E 20
Coburg St. EH6: Leith 5E 12
Cochrane Pl. EH6: Leith 6F 13
Cochran Ter. EH7: Edin 1H 21
Cochrina Pl. EH24: Rose 4D 46
Cockburn Cres. EH14: Bal 5D 36
Cockburnhill Rd. EH14: Bal ...6B 36
Cockburn St. EH1: Edin ...3H 21 (4E 4)
COCKENZIE 3G 15
Cockenzie Bus. Cen.
  EH32: Cock 3G 15
Cockmylane EH13: Edin 5D 32
Cockpen Av. EH19: Bonn 1G 47
Cockpen Cres. EH19: Bonn ...1G 47
Cockpen Dr. EH19: Bonn 1G 47
Cockpen Pl. EH19: Bonn 1G 47
Cockpen Rd. EH19: Bonn 7J 41
Cockpen Rd. Rdbt.
  EH19: Bonn 1K 47
Cockpen Ter. EH19: Bonn 1G 47
Cockpen Vw. EH19: Bonn 1G 47
Cock's Cft. EH12: Edin 6F 19
Coffin La. EH11: Edin 5D 20
Coillesdene Av. EH15: Port ...4K 23
Coillesdene Cres. EH15: Port .4K 23
Coillesdene Dr. EH15: Port ...4K 23
Coillesdene Gdns. EH15: Port .4K 23
Coillesdene Gro. EH15: Port ..4K 23
Coillesdene Ho. EH15: Port ...4K 23
Coillesdene Loan EH15: Port ..1A 24
Coillesdene Ter. EH15: Port ...4K 23
Coinyie Ho. Cl. EH1: Edin 4G 5
COLINTON 5K 31
Colinton Castle Sports Club ..4K 31
Colinton Gro. EH14: Edin 2B 32
Colinton Gro. W. EH14: Edin ..2B 32
Colinton Mains Cres.
  EH13: Edin 6C 32
Colinton Mains Dr.
  EH13: Edin 4B 32
Colinton Mains Gdns.
  EH13: Edin 4B 32
Colinton Mains Grn.
  EH13: Edin 5B 32
Colinton Mains Gro.
  EH13: Edin 5C 32
Colinton Mains Loan
  EH13: Edin 5B 32
Colinton Mains Pl.
  EH13: Edin 5C 32
Colinton Mains Rd.
  EH13: Edin 5B 32
Colinton Mains Ter.
  EH13: Edin 5C 32
Colinton Rd. EH10: Edin 1C 32
  EH13: Edin 5K 31
  EH14: Edin 3B 32
College Wynd
  EH1: Edin 4H 21 (5F 5)
Colliery Cres. EH22: Newt 2C 48
Colliery Vw. EH22: Newt 2D 48
Collins Pl. EH3: Edin 1F 21
Colmestone Ga. EH10: Edin ...6E 32
Coltbridge Av. EH12: Edin 4B 20
Coltbridge Gdns. EH12: Edin ..3C 20
Coltbridge Millside
  EH12: Edin 4C 20
  (off Coltbridge Av.)
Coltbridge Ter. EH12: Edin 4B 20
Coltbridge Va. EH12: Edin 4C 20
Columba Av. EH12: Edin 1K 19
Columba Rd. EH4: Edin 1K 19
Colville Pl. EH3: Edin 1F 21
COMELY BANK 1D 20
Comely Bank EH4: Edin 1D 20
Comely Bank Av. EH4: Edin ..1E 20
Comely Bank Gro. EH4: Edin ..1D 20
Comely Bank Pl. EH4: Edin ...1E 20
Comely Bank Pl. M.
  EH4: Edin 1E 20
Comely Bank Rd. EH4: Edin ..1E 20
Comely Bank Row EH4: Edin ..1E 20
Comely Bank St. EH4: Edin ...1D 20
Comely Bank Ter. EH4: Edin ..1E 20
Comely Grn. Cres. EH7: Edin ..2A 22
Comely Grn. Pl. EH7: Edin 2A 22
Comiston Dr. EH10: Edin 3D 32
Comiston Gdns. EH10: Edin ...2E 32
Comiston Gro. EH10: Edin 5E 32
Comiston Pl. EH10: Edin 2E 32

Comiston Ri. EH10: Edin 5E 32
Comiston Rd. EH10: Edin 4E 32
Comiston Springs Av.
  EH10: Edin 5E 32
Comiston Ter. EH10: Edin 4E 32
Comiston Vw. EH10: Edin 5E 32
Commercial St.
  EH6: Leith, Newh 4E 12
Commercial Wharf EH6: Leith ..4F 13
Conference Sq. EH3: Edin 6A 4
Conifer Rd. EH22: May 6G 43
Connaught Pl. EH6: Edin 5C 12
Considine Gdns. EH8: Edin 2C 22
Considine Ter. EH8: Edin 2C 22
Constitution St. EH6: Leith ...6F 13
Cook Cres. EH22: May 1F 49
Cookies Wynd EH32: Pres 6C 14
  (off Rope Wlk.)
Co-operative Bldgs.
  EH33: Tran 2H 27
Cooper's Cl. EH8: Edin 3H 5
Cope La. EH32: Port S 3G 15
Corbiehill Av. EH4: Edin 7D 10
Corbiehill Cres. EH4: Edin 7D 10
Corbiehill Gdns. EH4: Edin ...7D 10
Corbiehill Gro. EH4: Edin 7D 10
Corbiehill Pk. EH4: Edin 7C 10
Corbiehill Pl. EH4: Edin 7C 10
Corbiehill Rd. EH4: Edin 7C 10
Corbiehill Ter. EH4: Edin 7C 10
Corbieshot EH15: Edin 6H 23
Corbiewynd EH15: Edin 6H 23
Cornhill Ter. EH6: Leith 6G 13
Corn Market Village 1A 32
Cornwallis Pl. EH3: Edin 1G 21
Cornwall St. EH3: Edin 4F 21 (5B 4)
Coronation Pl. EH22: May 6F 43
  EH33: Tran 2G 27
Coronation Wlk.
  EH3: Edin 5G 21 (7D 4)
Corrennie Dr. EH10: Edin 2F 33
Corrennie Gdns. EH10: Edin ..3F 33
Corrie Ct. EH22: Newt 2D 48
Corslet Cres. EH14: Cur 7D 30
Corslet Pl. EH14: Cur 7C 30
Corslet Rd. EH14: Cur 7C 30
CORSTORPHINE 5F 19
Corstorphine Bank Av.
  EH12: Edin 4E 18
Corstorphine Bank Dr.
  EH12: Edin 4E 18
Corstorphine Bank Ter.
  EH12: Edin 4E 18
Corstorphine High St.
  EH12: Edin 5F 19
Corstorphine Hill Av.
  EH12: Edin 4G 19
Corstorphine Hill Cres.
  EH12: Edin 4G 19
Corstorphine Hill Gdns.
  EH12: Edin 4G 19
Corstorphine Hill Rd.
  EH12: Edin 4G 19
CORSTORPHINE HOSPITAL ...5H 19
Corstorphine Ho. Av.
  EH12: Edin 5G 19
Corstorphine Ho. Ter.
  EH12: Edin 5G 19
Corstorphine Pk. Gdns.
  EH12: Edin 5H 19
Corstorphine Rd. EH12: Edin ..5H 19
Cortleferry Dr. EH22: Dalk 4A 42
Cortleferry Gro. EH22: Dalk ...4A 42
Cortleferry Pk. EH22: Dalk 4A 42
Cortleferry Ter. EH22: Dalk ...4A 42
Corunna Pl. EH6: Edin 5E 12
Corunna Ter. EH26: Pen 6E 44
Costkea Way EH20: Loan 5A 40
Cotlaws EH29: Kltn 2A 16
Cottage Homes EH13: Edin ...6K 31
Cottage La. EH21: Muss 3G 25
Cottage Pk. EH4: Edin 2J 19
County Rd. EH32: Pres 6C 14
County Sq. EH32: Pres 6C 14
Couperfield EH6: Leith 4E 12
Couper St. EH6: Leith 4E 12
Cousland Rd. EH22: Dalk 1F 43
Covenanters La. EH30: S Q'fry ..1G 7
  (off High St.)
Cowan Rd. EH11: Edin 7C 20
Cowan's Cl. EH8: Edin ...5J 21 (7G 5)

Cowan Ter. EH26: Pen 7D 44
Cowden Cres. EH22: Dalk 2F 43
Cowden Gro. EH22: Dalk 2F 43
Cowden La. EH22: Dalk 2F 43
Cowden Pk. EH22: Dalk 2E 42
Cowden Ter. EH22: Dalk 2F 43
Cowden Vw. EH22: Dalk 2F 43
Cowgate EH1: Edin 4II 21 (5C 4)
Cowgatehead
  EH1: Edin 4H 21 (5E 4)
Cowpits EH21: Whit 6F 25
Cowpits Ford Rd. EH21: Muss ..5E 24
Cowpits Rd. EH21: Whit 6F 25
Coxfield EH11: Edin 6A 20
Crags Sports Cen. 4J 21 (6H 5)
Craigcrook Av. EH4: Edin 1H 19
Craigcrook Gdns. EH4: Edin ..2K 19
Craigcrook Gro. EH4: Edin ...2J 19
Craigcrook Pk. EH4: Edin 2J 19
Craigcrook Pl. EH4: Edin 2A 20
Craigcrook Rd. EH4: Edin 1H 19
Craigcrook Sq. EH4: Edin 1J 19
Craigcrook Ter. EH4: Edin 1A 20
Craigend Pk. EH16: Edin 3C 34
CRAIGENTINNY 1E 22
Craigentinny Av. EH7: Edin ...2E 22
Craigentinny Av. Nth.
  EH6: Edin 6J 13
Craigentinny Cres. EH7: Edin ..2E 22
Craigentinny Gro. EH7: Edin ..2E 22
Craigentinny Pl. EH7: Edin ...2E 22
Craigentinny Rd. EH7: Edin ...1D 22
Craighall Av. EH6: Newh 4B 12
Craighall Bank EH6: Newh 4B 12
Craighall Cres. EH6: Newh 4B 12
Craighall Gdns. EH6: Newh ...5B 12
Craighall Rd. EH6: Newh 4B 12
Craighall Ter. EH6: Newh 5B 12
  EH21: Muss 2H 25
Craighill Gdns. EH10: Edin ...3D 32
Craighouse Av. EH10: Edin ...2D 32
Craighouse Gdns. EH10: Edin ..2D 32
Craighouse Pk. EH10: Edin ...2D 32
Craighouse Rd. EH10: Edin ...2D 32
Craighouse Ter. EH10: Edin ..2D 32
Craigiebield Cres. EH26: Pen ..3C 50
Craigievar Ho. EH12: Edin 3D 18
Craigievar Sq. EH12: Edin 3D 18
Craigievar Wynd EH12: Edin ..4C 18
Craiglea Dr. EH10: Edin 3D 32
Craiglea Pl. EH10: Edin 3D 32
CRAIGLEITH 1B 20
Craigleith Av. Nth. EH4: Edin ..3A 20
Craigleith Av. Sth. EH4: Edin ..3A 20
Craigleith Bank EH4: Edin 2B 20
Craigleith Cres. EH4: Edin 2A 20
Craigleith Dr. EH4: Edin 2A 20
Craigleith Gdns. EH4: Edin ...2A 20
Craigleith Gro. EH4: Edin 2A 20
Craigleith Hill EH4: Edin 1B 20
Craigleith Hill Cres.
  EH4: Edin 1B 20
Craigleith Hill Gdns.
  EH4: Edin 1B 20
Craigleith Hill Grn. EH4: Edin ..1B 20
Craigleith Hill Gro. EH4: Edin ..1B 20
Craigleith Hill Loan
  EH4: Edin 1B 20
Craigleith Hill Pk. EH4: Edin ..1B 20
Craigleith Hill Row EH4: Edin ..1B 20
Craigleith Retail Pk.
  EH4: Edin 1B 20
Craigleith Ri. EH4: Edin 3A 20
Craigleith Rd. EH4: Edin 2B 20
Craigleith Vw. EH4: Edin 2A 20
CRAIGLOCKHART 3B 32
Craiglockhart Av. EH14: Edin ..2A 32
Craiglockhart Bank
  EH14: Edin 3A 32
Craiglockhart Castle (Remains of)
  ....3B 32
Craiglockhart Cres.
  EH14: Edin 3A 32
Craiglockhart Dell Rd.
  EH14: Edin 2A 32
Craiglockhart Dr. Nth.
  EH14: Edin 2A 32
Craiglockhart Dr. Sth.
  EH14: Edin 3A 32
Craiglockhart Gdns.
  EH14: Edin 2A 32

Craiglockhart Gro. EH14: Edin ..4A 32
Craiglockhart Loan
  EH14: Edin 3A 32
Craiglockhart Pk. EH14: Edin ..3A 32
Craiglockhart Pl. EH14: Edin ..2B 32
Craiglockhart Quad.
  EH14: Edin 3A 32
Craiglockhart Rd. EH14: Edin ..4A 32
Craiglockhart Rd. Nth.
  EH14: Edin 3B 32
  (not continuous)
Craiglockhart Sports Cen. 2B 32
Craiglockhart Tennis Cen. 2B 32
Craiglockhart Ter. EH14: Edin ..2C 32
Craiglockhart Vw. EH14: Edin ..2B 32
CRAIGMILLAR 1D 34
Craigmillar Castle 2D 34
Craigmillar Castle Av.
  EH16: Edin 1D 34
Craigmillar Castle Gdns.
  EH16: Edin 7D 22
Craigmillar Castle Loan
  EH16: Edin 7E 22
Craigmillar Castle Rd.
  EH16: Edin 7D 22
Craigmillar Ct. EH16: Edin ...1C 34
Craigmillar Pk. EH16: Edin ...1K 33
Craigmount App. EH12: Edin ..4E 18
Craigmount Av. EH12: Edin ...4E 18
Craigmount Av. Nth.
  EH4: Edin 2D 18
  EH12: Edin 2D 18
Craigmount Bank EH4: Edin ..2D 18
Craigmount Bank W.
  EH4: Edin 2D 18
Craigmount Brae EH12: Edin ..2D 18
Craigmount Ct. EH4: Edin 2D 18
Craigmount Cres. EH12: Edin ..3D 18
Craigmount Dr. EH12: Edin ...3D 18
Craigmount Gdns. EH12: Edin ..4D 18
Craigmount Gro. EH12: Edin ..4D 18
Craigmount Gro. Nth.
  EH12: Edin 3D 18
Craigmount Hill EH4: Edin ...2D 18
Craigmount Loan EH12: Edin ..3D 18
Craigmount Pk. EH12: Edin ...4D 18
Craigmount Pl. EH12: Edin ...4D 18
Craigmount Ter. EH12: Edin ..4D 18
Craigmount Vw. EH12: Edin ..3D 18
Craigmount Way EH12: Edin ..2E 18
Craigour Av. EH17: Edin 4E 34
Craigour Cres. EH17: Edin 4E 34
Craigour Dr. EH16: Edin 3D 34
Craigour Gdns. EH17: Edin ...4E 34
Craigour Grn. EH17: Edin 4D 34
Craigour Gro. EH17: Edin 4E 34
Craigour Loan EH17: Edin 4E 34
Craigour Pl. EH17: Edin 4D 34
Craigour Ter. EH17: Edin 4E 34
Craigpark Av. EH28: Rat 2C 28
Craigpark Cres. EH28: Rat 2C 28
Craigroyston Gro. EH4: Edin ..6D 10
Craigroyston Pl. EH4: Edin ...5D 10
Craigs Av. EH12: Edin 5D 18
Craigs Bank EH12: Edin 4D 18
Craig's Cl. EH1: Edin 4F 5
Craigs Cres. EH12: Edin 4D 18
Craigs Dr. EH12: Edin 4D 18
Craigs Gdns. EH12: Edin 4D 18
Craigs Gro. EH12: Edin 5E 18
Craigs Loan EH12: Edin 4E 18
Craigs Pk. EH12: Edin 4D 18
Craigs Rd. EH12: Edin 3K 17
Crame Ter. EH22: Dalk 3A 42
CRAMOND 4J 9
Cramond Av. EH4: Cram 5J 9
Cramond Bank EH4: Cram ...5J 9
CRAMOND BRIDGE 7G 9
Cramond Bri. Cotts.
  EH4: Cram 6G 9
Cramond Bri. Farm EH4: Cram ..7G 9
Cramond Brig Toll EH4: Cram ..6G 9
Cramond Cres. EH4: Cram 5J 9
Cramond Gdns. EH4: Cram ...5J 9
Cramond Glebe Gdns.
  EH4: Cram 4K 9
Cramond Glebe Rd. EH4: Cram ..4J 9
Cramond Glebe Ter. EH4: Cram ..4J 9
Cramond Grn. EH4: Cram 4J 9
Cramond Gro. EH4: Cram 5J 9
Cramond Pk. EH4: Cram 5J 9
Cramond Pl. EH4: Cram 5K 9

Gibson Ter.—Groathill Gdns. W.

Gibson Ter. EH11: Edin 5E **20**
Gifford Pk. EH8: Edin 5J **21** (7G **5**)
Gilberstoun EH15: Edin 5J **23**
Gilberstoun Brig EH15: Edin 6K **23**
Gilberstoun Loan EH15: Edin 6K **23**
Gilberstoun Pl. EH15: Edin 6K **23**
Gilberstoun Wynd
EH15: Edin 6K **23**
Giles St. EH6: Leith 5E **12**
Gillespie Cres. EH10: Edin 5F **21**
Gillespie Pl. EH3: Edin 5F **21** (7B **4**)
Gillespie Rd. EH13: Edin 6H **31**
Gillespie St. EH3: Edin 5F **21** (7A **4**)
Gillsland Gro. EH10: Edin 7D **20**
Gillsland Pk. EH10: Edin 7D **20**
Gillsland Rd. EH10: Edin 7D **20**
GILMERTON **6E 34**
Gilmerton Dykes Av.
EH17: Edin 7C **34**
Gilmerton Dykes Cres.
EH17: Edin 6C **34**
Gilmerton Dykes Dr.
EH17: Edin 6D **34**
Gilmerton Dykes Gdns.
EH17: Edin 6C **34**
Gilmerton Dykes Gro.
EH17: Edin 6C **34**
Gilmerton Dykes Loan
EH17: Edin 7D **34**
Gilmerton Dykes Pl.
EH17: Edin 6C **34**
Gilmerton Dykes Rd.
EH17: Edin 1D **40**
Gilmerton Dykes St.
EH17: Edin 7C **34**
Gilmerton Dykes Ter.
EH17: Edin 7D **34**
Gilmerton Dykes Vw.
EH17: Edin 7D **34**
Gilmerton Junc. **1G 41**
Gilmerton Pl. EH17: Edin 7D **34**
Gilmerton Rd. EH16: Edin 2A **34**
EH17: Edin 2A **34**
EH18: Edin 7F **35**
EH22: Dalk 2K **41**
Gilmerton Sta. Rd.
EH17: Edin 2E **40**
Gilmore Pk. EH3: Edin 5E **20**
Gilmore Pl. EH3: Edin 6E **20** (7A **4**)
Gilmore Pl. La.
EH3: Edin 5F **21** (7A **4**)
Gilmour Rd. EH16: Edin 1K **33**
Gilmour's Cl. EH1: Edin 5D **4**
Gilmour's Entry
EH8: Edin 4J **21** (6H **5**)
Gilmour St. EH8: Edin 4J **21** (6H **5**)
Girdle Wlk. EH32: Pres 6C **14**
Gladstone Pl. EH6: Edin 6G **13**
Gladstone's Land **4E 4**
Gladstone Ter. EH9: Edin 6J **21**
Glanville Pl. EH3: Edin 1A **4**
Glasgow Rd. EH12: Edin 6H **17**
EH28: Ing, Nbdge, Rat S 5B **16**
Glaskhill Ter. EH26: Pen 1C **50**
Glebe, The EH4: Cram 4J **9**
EH29: Kltn 1A **16**
EH30: Dalm 3K **7**
Glebe Gdns. EH12: Edin 5G **19**
EH32: Pres 6D **14**
Glebe Gro. EH12: Edin 5F **19**
Glebe Pl. EH18: Las 4F **41**
Glebe Rd. EH12: Edin 5F **19**
Glebe St. EH22: Dalk 2C **42**
Glebe Ter. EH12: Edin 5F **19**
Glenallan Dr. EH16: Edin 2B **34**
Glenallan Loan EH16: Edin 2B **34**
Glenalmond Ct. *EH11: Edin 2F 31*
(off Sighthill Bank)
GLENBROOK **5A 36**
Glenbrook EH14: Bal 5A **36**
Glenbrook Rd. EH14: Bal 5A **36**
Glencairn Cres. EH12: Edin 4D **20**
Glencorse Ho. EH4: Edin 7J **11**
Glencorse Pk. EH26: Mil B 6G **45**
Glencross Gdns. EH26: Pen 2A **50**
Glendevon Av. EH12: Edin 5K **19**
Glendevon Gdns. EH12: Edin 5J **19**
Glendevon Gro. EH12: Edin 5K **19**
Glendevon Pk. EH12: Edin 5K **19**
Glendevon Pl. EH12: Edin 5K **19**
Glendevon Rd. EH12: Edin 6K **19**
Glendevon Ter. EH12: Edin 5K **19**
Glendinning Cres. EH16: Edin 4A **34**
Glendinning Dr. EH29: Kltn 7E **6**
Glendinning Pl. EH29: Kltn 7E **6**
Glendinning Rd. EH29: Kltn 7E **6**
Glendinning Way EH29: Kltn 1A **16**
Glenesk Cres. EH22: Dalk 3B **42**
Glenfinlas St.
EH3: Edin 3F **21** (3A **4**)
Glengyle Ter.
EH3: Edin 5F **21** (7B **4**)
Glenisla Gdns. EH9: Edin 1H **33**
Glenisla Gdns. La. EH9: Edin 1H **33**
Glenlea Cotts. EH14: Edin 7A **20**
Glenlee Av. EH8: Edin 3C **22**
Glenlee Gdns. EH8: Edin 3C **22**
Glenlockhart Bank
EH14: Edin 3B **32**
Glenlockhart Rd. EH14: Edin 3B **32**
Glenlockhart Valley
EH14: Edin 2B **32**
Glennie Gdns. EH33: Tran 2H **27**
Glenogle Ho. EH3: Edin 1F **21**
Glenogle Pl. EH3: Edin 1F **21**
Glenogle Rd. EH3: Edin 1F **21**
Glenogle Swimming Cen. **1F 21**
Glenogle Ter. EH3: Edin 7A **12**
Glenorchy Ter. EH9: Edin 7K **21**
Glenpark EH14: Bal 4B **36**
Glen Pl. EH26: Pen 1C **50**
Glen St. EH3: Edin 5G **21** (6C **4**)
Glenure Loan EH4: Edin 2F **19**
Glenvarloch Cres. EH16: Edin 3B **34**
Glenview EH26: Pen 1C **50**
Glen Vw. Ct. EH23: Gore 6E **48**
Glen Vw. Cres. EH23: Gore 6E **48**
Glen Vw. Pl. EH23: Gore 7E **48**
Glen Vw. Rd. EH23: Gore 5E **48**
Glen Vw. Wlk. EH23: Gore 7F **49**
GLIMERTON DYKES **7D 34**
Gloucester La.
EH3: Edin 2F **21** (1A **4**)
Gloucester Pl.
EH3: Edin 2F **21** (1A **4**)
Gloucester Sq.
EH3: Edin 2F **21** (1A **4**)
Gloucester St.
EH3: Edin 2F **21** (1A **4**)
Goff Av. EH7: Edin 1F **23**
GOGAR **6K 17**
Gogarbank EH12: Edin 2K **29**
Gogar Bri. Rd. EH12: Edin A 4G **17**
Gogar Junc. **5A 18**
Gogarloch Bank EH12: Edin 6D **18**
Gogarloch Haugh EH12: Edin 6D **18**
Gogarloch Muir EH12: Edin 6D **18**
Gogarloch Rd. EH12: Edin 6C **18**
Gogarloch Syke EH12: Edin 6C **18**
Gogar Mains Farm Rd.
EH12: Edin 4J **17**
Gogar Pk. Curling Rink **6A 18**
Gogar Sta. Rd. EH12: Edin 6K **17**
EH14: Cur 2B **30**
Gogarstone Rd. EH28: Ing 6H **17**
GOLDENACRE **6A 12**
Goldenacre **6A 12**
Goldenacre Ter. EH3: Edin 6A **12**
Golf Course Rd. EH19: Bonn 5H **41**
Golf Dr. EH32: Port S 3J **15**
GOOSE GREEN **1F 25**
Goose Grn. Av. EH21: Muss 1F **25**
Goose Grn. Bri. EH21: Muss 1E **24**
Goose Grn. Cres. EH21: Muss 1F **25**
Goose Grn. Pl. EH21: Muss 1F **25**
Goose Grn. Rd. EH21: Muss 1F **25**
Gordon Av. EH19: Bonn 7F **41**
Gordon Ct. EH6: Edin 6F **13**
Gordon Loan EH12: Edin 4G **19**
Gordon Rd. EH12: Edin 4G **19**
Gordon St. EH6: Edin 6E **12**
EH22: East 6E **42**
Gordon Ter. EH16: Edin 2A **34**
Gore Av. EH23: Gore 6E **48**
GOREBRIDGE **6F 49**
Gorebridge Leisure Cen. 6E **48**
GORGIE **7C 20**
Gorgie Pk. Cl. EH14: Edin 7B **20**
Gorgie Pk. Rd. EH11: Edin 6B **20**
Gorgie Rd. EH11: Edin 1J **31**
Gorton Av. EH18: Las 3D **46**
Gorton Loan EH24: Rose 4D **46**
Gorton Pl. EH24: Rose 4D **46**
Gorton Rd. EH24: Rose 4D **46**
Gorton Wlk. EH24: Rose 4D **46**
Goschen Ho. *EH10: Edin 7E 20*
(off Blantyre Ter.)
Gosford Pl. EH6: Edin 5C **12**
Gosford Rd. EH32: Port S 3G **15**
Gosford Wlk. *EH32: Port S 3G 15*
(off Gosford Rd.)
Gospel Wynd EH18: Las 4G **41**
Goto La. EH30: S Q'fry 1H **7**
Gowanhill Farm Rd.
EH14: Cur 7H **29**
Gowkley Moss Rdbt.
EH26: Mil B 3H **45**
Gowkshill Farm Cotts.
EH23: Gore 3D **48**
Gracefield Ct. EH21: Muss 2D **24**
GRACEMOUNT **6B 34**
Gracemount Av. EH16: Edin 5B **34**
Gracemount Bus. Pav.
EH16: Edin 7C **34**
Gracemount Dr. EH16: Edin 6B **34**
Gracemount Leisure Cen. **7B 34**
Gracemount Pl. EH16: Edin 6B **34**
Gracemount Rd. EH16: Edin 7A **34**
Gracemount Sq. EH16: Edin 5B **34**
Graham's Rd. EH26: Mil B 5F **45**
Graham St. EH6: Edin 5D **12**
Granby Rd. EH16: Edin 1K **33**
Grandfield EH6: Newh 5B **12**
Grandville EH6: Newh 4B **12**
GRANGE, THE **7H 21**
Grange Ct. *EH9: Edin 6J 21*
(off Causewayside)
Grange Cres. EH9: Edin 7H **21**
Grange Cres. E. EH32: Pres 6D **14**
Grange Cres. W. EH32: Pres 6D **14**
Grange Gro. EH32: Pres 6D **14**
Grange Loan EH9: Edin 7G **21**
Grange Loan Gdns. EH9: Edin 7H **21**
Grange Rd. EH9: Edin 6H **21**
EH32: Pres 6D **14**
Grange Ter. EH9: Edin 1H **33**
Grannies Pk. Ind. Est.
EH22: Dalk 1C **42**
Grannus M. EH21: Muss 3F **25**
Grant Av. EH13: Edin 6J **31**
GRANTON **4H 11**
Granton Cres. EH5: Edin 4H **11**
Granton Gdns. EH5: Edin 4J **11**
Granton Gro. EH5: Edin 4J **11**
Granton Mains Av. EH4: Edin 4F **11**
Granton Mains Bank
EH4: Edin 4F **11**
Granton Mains Brae
EH4: Edin 5F **11**
Granton Mains Ct. EH4: Edin 5G **11**
Granton Mains E. EH4: Edin 4G **11**
Granton Mains Gait EH4: Edin 4F **11**
Granton Mains Va. EH4: Edin 4F **11**
Granton Mains Wynd
EH4: Edin 4F **11**
Granton Medway EH5: Edin 4H **11**
Granton Mill Cres. EH4: Edin 4F **11**
Grantonmill Dr. EH4: Edin 4F **11**
Granton Mill March
EH4: Edin 5E **10**
Granton Mill Pk. EH4: Edin 5E **10**
Granton Mill Pl. EH4: Edin 5E **10**
Granton Mill Rd. EH4: Edin 4E **10**
Granton Pk. Av. EH5: Edin 3H **11**
Granton Pier EH5: Edin 3J **11**
Granton Pl. EH5: Edin 4J **11**
Granton Rd. EH5: Edin 4J **11**
Granton Shop. Pk., The
EH5: Edin 3J **11**
Granton Sq. EH5: Edin 3J **11**
Granton Ter. EH5: Edin 4J **11**
Granton Vw. EH5: Edin 4J **11**
Grantully Pl. EH9: Edin 7K **21**
Granville Ter. EH10: Edin 6E **20**
Grassmarket
EH1: Edin 4G **21** (5D **4**)
Gray's Ct. EH8: Edin 4J **21** (6G **5**)
Graysknowe *EH14: Edin 2K 31*
(off Inglis Grn. Rd.)
Grays Loan EH10: Edin 7D **20**
Gt. Cannon Bank EH15: Port 2G **23**
Gt. Carleton Pl. EH16: Edin 1G **35**
Gt. Carleton Sq. EH16: Edin 1G **35**
Gt. Junction St. EH6: Edin 5E **12**
Gt. King St. EH3: Edin 2G **21** (1C **4**)
Gt. Michael Ri. EH6: Newh 4C **12**
Gt. Michael Sq. *EH6: Newh 3C 12*
(off Newhaven Pl.)
Gt. Stuart St.
EH3: Edin 3E **20** (3A **4**)
Green, The EH4: Edin 6C **10**
EH14: Bal 5F **37**
EH20: Loan 4C **40**
Greenacre EH14: Edin 4F **31**
GREENBANK **4D 32**
Greenbank Av. EH10: Edin 3E **32**
Greenbank Cres. EH10: Edin 5D **32**
Greenbank Dr. EH10: Edin 4C **32**
Greenbank Gdns. EH10: Edin 4D **32**
Greenbank Gro. EH10: Edin 4D **32**
Greenbank La. EH10: Edin 3D **32**
Greenbank Loan EH10: Edin 4D **32**
Greenbank Pk. EH10: Edin 4D **32**
Greenbank Pl. EH10: Edin 3E **32**
Greenbank Ri. EH10: Edin 5D **32**
Greenbank Rd. EH10: Edin 4D **32**
Greenbank Row EH10: Edin 4D **32**
Greenbank Ter. EH10: Edin 3E **32**
Greendale Pk. EH4: Edin 6D **10**
GREENDYKES **1F 35**
Greendykes Av. EH16: Edin 1F **35**
Greendykes Dr. EH16: Edin 1F **35**
Greendykes Gdns. EH16: Edin 1F **35**
Greendykes Ho. EH16: Edin 1F **35**
Greendykes Loan EH16: Edin 1F **35**
Greendykes Rd. EH16: Edin 7F **23**
Greendykes Ter. EH16: Edin 1F **35**
GREENEND **4C 34**
Greenend Dr. EH17: Edin 4C **34**
Greenend Gdns. EH17: Edin 4C **34**
Greenend Gro. EH17: Edin 4C **34**
Greenfield Cres. EH14: Bal 5E **36**
Greenfield Pk. EH21: Muss 5D **24**
Greenfield Rd. EH14: Bal 5E **36**
Greenhall Cres. EH23: Gore 5E **48**
Greenhall Rd. EH23: Gore 5E **48**
GREENHILL **7F 21**
Greenhill Ct. EH9: Edin 6F **21**
Greenhill Gdns. EH10: Edin 6F **21**
Greenhill Pk. EH10: Edin 7F **21**
EH26: Pen 2B **50**
Greenhill Pl. EH10: Edin 7F **21**
Greenhill Ter. EH10: Edin 6F **21**
Green La. EH18: Las 5F **41**
Greenlaw Gro. EH26: Mil B 5E **44**
Greenlaw Hedge EH13: Edin 4C **32**
GREENLAW MAINS **6E 44**
Greenlaw Rig EH13: Edin 4C **32**
Greenmantle Loan
EH16: Edin 3B **34**
Green Pk. EH17: Edin 4C **34**
Greens Health & Fitness **1K 31**
GREENSIDE **2J 21** (1G **5**)
Greenside End
EH7: Edin 2J **21** (1G **5**)
Greenside La.
EH1: Edin 2J **21** (1G **5**)
Greenside Pl. EH1: Edin 1G **5**
EH24: Rose 4D **46**
Greenside Row
EH1: Edin 2J **21** (2G **5**)
Green St. EH7: Edin 1H **21**
Greenway, The EH14: Edin 3G **31**
(Hailesland Rd.)
EH14: Edin 4F **31**
(Murrayburn Pl.)
Greyfriars EH1: Edin 4H **21** (5E **4**)
Greyfriars Bobby **5E 4**
Greyfriars Pl. EH1: Edin 5E **4**
Grey School Cnr.
EH32: Pres 6D **14**
Grierson Av. EH5: Edin 4K **11**
Grierson Cres. EH5: Edin 4K **11**
Grierson Gdns. EH5: Edin 4K **11**
Grierson Rd. EH5: Edin 4J **11**
Grierson Sq. EH5: Edin 4K **11**
Grierson Vs. EH5: Edin 4K **11**
Grieve Ct. EH26: Pen 7D **44**
Grigor Av. EH4: Edin 7G **11**
Grigor Dr. EH4: Edin 7G **11**
Grigor Gdns. EH4: Edin 7G **11**
Grigor Ter. EH4: Edin 7G **11**
Grindlay St. EH3: Edin 4F **21** (5B **4**)
Grindlay St. Ct.
EH3: Edin 4F **21** (6B **4**)
Groathill Av. EH4: Edin 1A **20**
Groathill Gdns. E. EH4: Edin 1A **20**
Groathill Gdns. W. EH4: Edin 1A **20**

House o'Hill Row—Kirkliston

House o'Hill Row EH4: Edin 7E 10
House o'Hill Ter. EH4: Edin 1K 19
Howard Pl. EH3: Edin 7B 12
Howard St. EH3: Edin 7B 12
Howden Hall Cotts.
EH16: Edin 6A 34
Howden Hall Ct. EH16: Edin 6K 33
Howden Hall Cres.
EH16: Edin 7K 33
Howden Hall Dr. EH16: Edin 6K 33
Howden Hall Gdns.
EH16: Edin 6A 34
Howden Hall Loan
EH16: Edin 6K 33
Howden Hall Pk. EH16: Edin 6K 33
Howden Hall Rd. EH16: Edin . . .6A 34
Howden Hall Way EH16: Edin . . .7A 34
Howden St. EH8: Edin . . .5J 21 (6G 5)
Howe Pk. EH10: Edin 7D 32
Howe St. EH3: Edin 2G 21 (1C 4)
Hub, The 4E 4
Hughes Cres. EH22: May 7H 43
Hugh Miller Pl. EH3: Edin 1F 21
Hugh Russell Pl.
EH30: S Q'fry 2G 7
Huly Hill Rd. EH28: Nbdge 6A 16
Humbie Rd. EH29: Kltn 1A 16
Hungerage Sq. EH33: Tran 3H 27
Hunt Cl. EH22: Dalk 1C 42
Hunter Av. EH20: Loan 5D 40
Hunter Ct. EH20: Loan 5D 40
HUNTERFIELD 5E 48
Hunterfield Ct. EH23: Gore 6E 48
Hunterfield Pk. EH23: Gore 5E 48
Hunterfield Rd. EH23: Gore 5E 48
Hunterfield Ter. EH23: Gore 5D 48
Hunter's Cl. EH1: Edin 5D 4
Hunter's Hill EH26: Pen 1A 50
Hunter Sq. EH1: Edin 3H 21 (4F 5)
EH23: Gore 7F 49
Hunter Ter. EH19: Bonn 6H 41
EH20: Loan 5D 40
Huntingdon Pl. EH7: Edin 1J 21
Huntly St. EH3: Edin 7B 12
Hursted Av. EH22: East 6F 43
Hutchison Av. EH14: Edin 1A 32
Hutchison Cotts. EH14: Edin 1A 32
Hutchison Crossway
EH14: Edin 7A 20
(not continuous)
Hutchison Gdns. EH14: Edin 1A 32
Hutchison Gro. EH14: Edin 1B 32
Hutchison Ho. EH14: Edin 7B 20
Hutchison Loan EH14: Edin 1A 32
Hutchison Medway
EH14: Edin 1A 32
Hutchison Pk. EH14: Edin 7A 20
Hutchison Pl. EH14: Edin 1A 32
Hutchison Rd. EH14: Edin 1A 32
Hutchison Ter. EH14: Edin 1A 32
Hutchison Vw. EH14: Edin 7A 20
Hyndford's Cl. EH1: Edin 4G 5
Hyvot Av. EH17: Edin 6D 34
Hyvot Bank Av. EH17: Edin 6E 34
Hyvot Ct. EH17: Edin 7D 34
Hyvot Gdns. EH17: Edin 6D 34
Hyvot Grn. EH17: Edin 7D 34
Hyvot Gro. EH17: Edin 6D 34
Hyvot Loan EH17: Edin 6D 34
Hyvot Pk. EH17: Edin 7D 34
HYVOTS BANK 6D 34
Hyvot Ter. EH17: Edin 6D 34
Hyvot Vw. EH17: Edin 7D 34

I

Imex Bus. Cen. EH20: Loan 6A 40
Imrie Pl. EH26: Pen 2D 50
INCH .3B 34
Inchcolm Ct. EH4: Edin 5F 11
Inchcolm Ter. EH30: S Q'fry 2G 7
Inch Garvie Ct. EH4: Edin 6F 11
Inchgarvie Pk. EH30: S Q'fry 1F 7
Inchkeith Av. EH30: S Q'fry 2H 7
Inchkeith Ct. EH7: Edin 7D 12
Inchkeith Gro. EH33: Tran 1H 27
Inchmickery Ct. EH4: Edin 5D 10
Inch Vw. EH32: Pres 6C 14
Inchview Cres. EH21: Wall 3A 26
Inchview Nth. EH32: Pres 6B 14
Inchview Rd. EH21: Wall 3K 25
Inchview Ter. EH7: Edin 2F 23
India Bldgs. EH1: Edin 5E 4
India Pl. EH3: Edin 2F 21 (1A 4)
India St. EH3: Edin 2F 21 (1B 4)
Industrial Rd. EH6: Edin 6G 13
Industry Homes EH6: Newh 5D 12
Industry La. EH6: Newh 5D 12
Infirmary St. EH1: Edin . . .4J 21 (5G 5)
Inglewood Pl. EH16: Edin 4B 34
Inglis Av. EH32: Port S 3G 15
Inglis Ct. EH1: Edin 5D 4
Inglis Farm EH32: Cock 4G 15
Inglis Grn. Gait EH14: Edin 2K 31
Inglis Grn. Rigg EH14: Edin 2K 31
Inglis Grn. Rd. EH14: Edin 2K 31
Ingliston Cotts. EH28: Ing 4E 16
Ingliston Rd. EH28: Ing 4E 16
Inkerman Ct. EH26: Pen 6E 44
Inveralmond Dr. EH4: Cram 5H 9
Inveralmond Gdns. EH4: Cram . . .5H 9
Inveralmond Gro. EH4: Cram 5H 9
Inveravon Rd. EH20: Loan 4B 40
Inveravon Ter. EH21: Muss 3E 24
INVERESK 4F 25
Inveresk Brae EH21: Muss 3F 25
Inveresk Est., The
EH21: Muss 4E 24
Inveresk Ga. EH21: Muss 3F 25
Inveresk Ind. Est.
EH21: Muss 3E 24
Inveresk Lodge Garden 4F 25
Inveresk Mills Ind. Pk.
EH21: Muss 4D 24
Inveresk Rd. EH21: Muss 3E 24
Inveresk Village EH21: Muss . . .3E 24
Inveresk Village Rd.
EH21: Muss 3F 25
INVERLEITH 7J 11
Inverleith 6K 11
Inverleith Av. EH5: Edin 6A 12
Inverleith Av. Sth. EH3: Edin 6A 12
Inverleith Gdns. EH3: Edin 6K 11
Inverleith Gro. EH3: Edin 7J 11
Inverleith House 7K 11
Inverleith Pl. EH3: Edin 7J 11
Inverleith Pl. La. EH3: Edin 6A 12
Inverleith Row EH3: Edin 6A 12
Inverleith Ter. EH3: Edin 7A 12
Inverleith Ter. La. EH3: Edin 7A 12
Iona St. EH6: Edin 7E 12
Ironmills Rd. EH22: Dalk 2B 42
Ivanhoe Cres. EH16: Edin 3B 34
Ivy Ter. EH11: Edin 6C 20

J

Jack Kane Cen., The 7G 23
Jackson's Cl. EH1: Edin 4F 5
Jackson's Entry EH8: Edin 3J 5
Jackson St. EH26: Pen 2C 50
Jacobite Way EH32: Pres 6F 15
Jacobs Way EH23: Gore 6E 48
Jamaica M. EH3: Edin 1B 4
Jamaica St. EH3: Edin . . .2F 21 (1B 4)
(not continuous)
Jamaica St. Nth. La.
EH3: Edin 2F 21 (1B 4)
Jamaica St. Sth. La.
EH3: Edin 2F 21 (1B 4)
James' Ct. EH1: Edin 4E 4
James Craig Wlk. EH1: Edin 2F 5
James Lean Av. EH22: Dalk 2D 42
James Leary Way EH19: Bonn . . .5J 41
Jameson Pl. EH6: Edin 7E 12
James St. EH15: Port 3J 23
EH21: Muss 2F 25
James St. La. EH15: Port 3J 23
Janefield EH17: Edin 1A 40
Jane St. EH6: Edin 6E 12
Jane Ter. EH7: Edin 2A 22
Jarnac Ct. *EH22: Dalk 2C 42*
(off High St.)
Jawbone Wlk.
EH3: Edin 5H 21 (7E 4)
Jean Armour Av. EH16: Edin 3A 34
Jean Armour Dr. EH22: Dalk 3F 43
Jeanette Stewart Dr.
EH22: Newt 2B 48
Jeffrey Av. EH4: Edin 2K 19
Jeffrey St. EH1: Edin 3J 21 (3F 5)
Jenks Loan EH22: Newt 1C 48
Jessfield Ter. EH6: Newh 4C 12
Jewel, The EH15: Edin 6H 23
JOCKS LODGE 2D 22
Jocks Lodge EH8: Edin 2C 22
John Bernard Way
EH23: Gore 7E 48
John Cres. EH33: Tran 2G 27
John Humble St. EH22: May 1G 49
John Kerr Ct. EH11: Edin 6D 20
John Knox House 3J 21 (4G 5)
John Knox Pl. EH26: Pen 2D 50
John Mason Ct. EH30: S Q'fry . . .2H 7
Johnnie Cope's Rd.
EH32: Pres 7E 14
EH33: Tran 1E 26
Johnny Moat Pl. EH32: Pres 6D 14
Johnsburn Grn. EH14: Bal 4D 36
Johnsburn Haugh EH14: Bal 4D 36
Johnsburn Pk. EH14: Bal 5D 36
Johnsburn Rd. EH14: Bal 4D 36
John's La. EH6: Leith 5F 13
John's Pl. EH6: Leith 5F 13
Johnston Pl. EH26: Pen 6D 44
Johnston Ter.
EH1: Edin 4G 21 (5C 4)
EH32: Port S 3H 15
John St. EH15: Port 3J 23
EH26: Pen 1C 50
John St. La. EH15: Port 3J 23
EH26: Pen 2C 50
John St. La. E. EH15: Port 3J 23
John St. La. W. EH15: Port 3J 23
JOPPA 4J 23
Joppa Gdns. EH15: Port 4J 23
Joppa Gro. EH15: Port 4J 23
Joppa Pans EH15: Port 1A 24
Joppa Pk. EH15: Port 3J 23
Joppa Rd. EH15: Port 4J 23
Joppa Sta. Pl.
EH15: Port 4J 23
Joppa Ter. EH15: Port 4J 23
Jordan La. EH10: Edin 1F 33
Jubilee Cres. EH23: Gore 5E 48
Jubilee Rd. EH12: Edin A 3F 17
Junction Pl. EH6: Edin 6E 12
Juner Pl. EH23: Gore 5E 48
Juniper Av. EH14: J Grn 6E 30
Juniper Gdns. EH14: J Grn 6E 30
JUNIPER GREEN 6F 31
Juniper Gro. EH14: J Grn 6E 30
Juniper La. EH14: J Grn 6F 31
Juniperlee EH14: J Grn 6F 31
Juniper Pk. Rd. EH14: J Grn 6F 31
Juniper Pl. EH14: J Grn 7E 30
Juniper Ter. EH14: J Grn 6E 30

K

KAIMES 7A 34
Kaimes Rd. EH12: Edin 4G 19
Kaimes Vw. EH22: Dan 5H 35
Katesmill Rd. EH14: Edin 4J 31
Kay Gdns. EH32: Cock 3G 15
Kedslie Pl. EH16: Edin 5K 33
Kedslie Rd. EH16: Edin 5K 33
Keir Hardie Dr. EH22: May 1G 49
Keir St. EH3: Edin 4G 21 (6D 4)
Keith Cres. EH4: Edin 2K 19
Keith Ho. EH12: Edin 7C 18
Keith Row EH4: Edin 2A 20
Keith Ter. EH4: Edin 2K 19
Kekewich Av. EH7: Edin 1F 23
Kemp Pl. EH3: Edin 1F 21
Kempston Pl. EH30: S Q'fry 2H 7
Kenilworth Dr. EH16: Edin 4A 34
Kenmure Av. EH8: Edin 3C 22
Kennedy Cres. EH33: Tran 1H 27
Kennington Av. EH20: Loan 6B 40
Kennington Ter. EH20: Loan 5B 40
Kerr Av. EH22: Dalk 3A 42
Kerr-McNeill Service Rd.
EH33: Tran 3G 27
(off King's Rd.)
Kerr Rd. EH33: Tran 2G 27
Kerr St. EH3: Edin 1F 21 (1A 4)
Kerr's Wynd EH21: Muss 2F 25
Kerr Way EH33: Tran 2G 27
Kevock Rd. EH18: Las 5F 41
Kevock Va. Cvn. Pk.
EH18: Las 5G 41
Kew Ter. EH12: Edin 4C 20
Kilchurn Ct. *EH12: Edin 4C 18*
(off Craigievar Wynd)
Kilgraston Ct. EH9: Edin 7G 21
Kilgraston Rd. EH9: Edin 7H 21
Kilmaurs Rd. EH16: Edin 7A 22
Kilmaurs Ter. EH16: Edin 7A 22
Kilncroftside EH14: Edin 2K 31
Kilngate Brae EH17: Edin 7D 34
Kilwinning Pl. EH21: Muss 2E 24
Kilwinning St. EH21: Muss 2F 25
Kilwinning Ter. EH21: Muss 2F 25
Kimmerghame Ho.
EH4: Edin 7H 11
Kincaid's Ct. EH1: Edin 5F 5
Kinellan Gdns. EH12: Edin 4A 20
Kinellan Rd. EH12: Edin 3A 20
King Edward VII Memorial 3K 5
King Edward's Way
EH29: Kltn 2A 16
Kinghorn Pl. EH6: Edin 5C 12
King Malcolm Cl. EH10: Edin . . .7H 33
Kingsburgh Rd. EH12: Edin 4A 20
Kings Cramond EH4: Cram 6J 9
KINGS GATE JUNC. 1A 42
Kings Haugh EH16: Edin 7C 22
KINGSKNOWE 3J 31
Kingsknowe Av. EH14: Edin 4J 31
Kingsknowe Ct. EH14: Edin 3H 31
Kingsknowe Cres. EH14: Edin . . .3J 31
Kingsknowe Dr. EH14: Edin 3J 31
Kingsknowe Gdns. EH14: Edin . . .4J 31
Kingsknowe Gro. EH14: Edin 4J 31
Kingsknowe Pk. EH14: Edin 4J 31
Kingsknowe Pl. EH14: Edin 3H 31
Kingsknowe Rd. Nth.
EH14: Edin 2J 31
Kingsknowe Rd. Sth.
EH14: Edin 3J 31
Kingsknowe Station (Rail) 3J 31
Kingsknowe Ter. EH14: Edin 3J 31
Kingslaw Ct. EH33: Tran 3H 27
King's Mdw. EH16: Edin 7B 22
King's Pl. EH15: Port 1G 23
King's Rd. EH15: Port 2G 23
EH33: Tran 3G 27
King's Stables La.
EH1: Edin 4G 21 (5C 4)
King's Stables Rd.
EH1: Edin 3F 21 (4B 4)
King's Ter. EH15: Port 1G 23
King's Theatre 5F 21 (7C 4)
Kingston Av. EH16: Edin 3C 34
King St. EH6: Leith 5E 12
EH21: Muss 3F 25
Kinleith Ind. Est. EH14: Cur 1K 37
Kinnaird Pk. EH15: Edin 7J 23
Kinnear Rd. EH3: Edin 6J 11
Kippielaw Dr. EH22: East 3E 42
Kippielaw Gdns. EH22: East 4E 42
Kippielaw Medway
EH22: East 4E 42
Kippielaw Pk. EH22: May 5F 43
Kippielaw Rd. EH22: East 4E 42
Kippielaw Steading
EH22: Dalk 4E 42
Kippielaw Wlk. EH22: East 3E 42
Kirk Brae EH16: Edin 3A 34
EH26: Mil B 4F 45
Kirk Cramond EH4: Cram 4J 9
Kirkgate EH6: Leith 5E 12
EH14: Cur 1J 37
EH16: Edin 5A 34
Kirkgate Ho. EH6: Leith 5F 13
KIRKHILL 1E 50
Kirkhill Ct. EH23: Gore 7E 48
Kirkhill Dr. EH16: Edin 7A 22
Kirkhill Gdns. EH16: Edin 6A 22
EH26: Pen 2D 50
Kirkhill Rd. EH16: Edin 6A 22
EH26: Pen 2D 50
Kirkhill Ter. EH16: Edin 6A 22
EH23: Gore 5C 48
Kirkhill Way EH26: Pen 2D 50
Kirklands EH12: Edin 7F 19
EH26: Pen 2C 50
Kirklands Pk. Cres. EH29: Kltn . . .7E 6
Kirklands Pk. Gdns.
EH29: Kltn 1A 16
Kirklands Pk. Gro. EH29: Kltn . . .1A 16
Kirklands Pk. Rigg EH29: Kltn . . .1A 16
Kirklands Pk. St. EH29: Kltn 1A 16
KIRKLISTON 1A 16

Long Craig Rigg—Megabowl

Long Craig Rigg EH5: Edin 3F 11
Longcraig Rd. EH30: S Q'fry 1J 7
Long Craigs EH32: Port S 3J 15
Long Crook EH30: S Q'fry 2F 7
Long Dalmahoy Rd.
EH14: Cur 7K 29
EH27: Kntn 1A 36
Longdykes EH32: Pres 5E 14
Longdykes Rd. EH32: Pres 5F 15
Longformacus Rd.
EH16: Edin 5A 34
LONGSTONE 2J 31
Longstone Av. EH14: Edin 2J 31
Longstone Cotts. EH14: Edin 2J 31
Longstone Cres. EH14: Edin 1J 31
Longstone Gdns. EH14: Edin 1H 31
Longstone Gro. EH14: Edin 2J 31
Longstone Pk. EH14: Edin 2J 31
Longstone Rd. EH14: Edin 1H 31
Longstone St. EH14: Edin 2J 31
Longstone Ter. EH14: Edin 1H 31
Longstone Vw. EH14: Edin 1H 31
Lonsdale Ter.
EH3: Edin 5G 21 (7C 4)
Lord Russell Pl. *EH9: Edin 6J 21*
(off Sciennes Pl.)
Loretto Ct. EH21: Muss 4D 24
Lorimer Vw. EH14: J Grn 6G 31
Lorne Gro. EH20: Loan 4A 40
Lorne Ho. EH3: Edin 3E 20
Lorne Pl. EH6: Edin 7E 12
Lorne Sq. EH6: Edin 7E 12
Lorne St. EH6: Edin 7E 12
Lothian Bank EH22: Dalk 4B 42
LOTHIANBRIDGE 7C 42
LOTHIANBURN 2G 39
Lothianburn Junc. 1F 39
Lothian Dr. EH22: East 5E 42
Lothian Rd. EH1: Edin 3F 21 (4A 4)
EH3: Edin 4F 21 (4A 4)
EH22: Dalk 2C 42
Lothian St. EH1: Edin 4H 21 (6F 5)
EH19: Bonn 6H 41
EH22: Dalk 2C 42
EH24: Rose 4D 46
Lothian Ter. EH22: Newt 2D 48
Lothian Thistle FC 7K 19
Louisa Sq. EH24: Rose 4D 46
Lovedale Av. EH14: Bal 4D 36
Lovedale Cres. EH14: Bal 4D 36
Lovedale Gdns. EH14: Bal 4E 36
Lovedale Gro. EH14: Bal 4D 36
Lovedale Rd. EH14: Bal 4E 36
Lover's La. EH30: S Q'fry 2H 7
(not continuous)
Lover's Loan EH9: Edin 6H 21
Lower Broomieknowe
EH18: Las 5G 41
Lwr. Gilmore Pl.
EH3: Edin 5F 21 (7A 4)
Lwr. Granton Rd. EH5: Edin 3J 11
Lower Joppa EH15: Port 3J 23
Lwr. London Rd. EH7: Edin 2A 22
Lwr. Valleyfield Vw.
EH26: Pen 3D 50
Lowrie Av. EH26: Pen 2A 50
Lowrie's Den Rd. EH26: Pen 2A 50
Lufra Bank EH5: Edin 4K 11
Lugton Brae EH22: Dalk 1B 42
Lumsden Ct. EH28: Rat 2D 28
Lussielaw Rd. EH9: Edin 2J 33
Lutton Pl. EH8: Edin 5J 21
Lygon Rd. EH16: Edin 2K 33
Lyndene Sq. EH20: Loan 4K 39
Lynedoch Pl. EH3: Edin 3E 20
Lynedoch Pl. La. EH3: Edin 3E 20
Lyne St. EH7: Edin 2A 22 (1K 5)
Lyne Ter. EH26: Pen 7E 44
Lyon's Cl. EH1: Edin 4F 5

M

Macbeth Moir Rd.
EH21: Muss 2J 25
McCathie Dr. EH22: Newt 7D 42
MacCormick Ter. EH26: Pen 6D 44
McDiarmid Gro. EH22: Newt 2D 48
McDonald Pl. EH7: Edin 7C 12
McDonald Rd. EH7: Edin 7C 12
McDonald St. EH7: Edin 7D 12
Macdowall Rd. EH9: Edin 1J 33
Macfarlane Ct. EH33: Elph 7F 27
McGahey Ct. EH22: Newt 2D 48
McKelvie Pde. EH5: Edin 3A 12
Mackenzie Pl.
EH3: Edin 2E 20 (1A 4)
Mackies Way *EH32: Pres 6C 14*
(off Inch Vw.)
McKinlay Ter. EH20: Loan 6A 40
McKinnon Dr. EH22: May 2G 49
McLaren Rd. EH9: Edin 7A 22
McLaren Ter. EH11: Edin 4E 20
McLean Pl. EH18: Las 7E 40
EH23: Gore 5F 49
McLean Wlk. EH22: Newt 2D 48
McLeod Cres. EH32: Pres 6D 14
McLeod St. EH11: Edin 5C 20
McNeill Av. EH20: Loan 5B 40
McNeill Path EH33: Tran 2G 27
McNeill Pl. EH20: Loan 5B 40
McNeill St. EH11: Edin 5E 20
McNeill Ter. EH20: Loan 6A 40
McNeill Wlk. EH33: Tran 3G 27
McNeill Way EH33: Tran 3G 27
McPhail Sq. EH33: Tran 2H 27
McQuade St. EH19: Bonn 5K 41
Mactaggart Loan EH22: Newt 2D 48
Madeira Pl. EH6: Newh 5D 12
Madeira St. EH6: Newh 4D 12
Maesterton Pl. EH22: Newt 2D 48
Magdala Cres. EH12: Edin 4D 20
Magdala M. EH12: Edin 4D 20
Magdalen Chapel 5E 4
MAGDALENE 5H 23
Magdalene Av. EH15: Port 5H 23
Magdalene Cotts. EH21: Port 1B 24
Magdalene Ct. EH15: Port 6H 23
Magdalene Dr. EH15: Port 5G 23
Magdalene Gdns. EH15: Port 5H 23
Magdalene Loan EH15: Port 5H 23
Magdalene Medway
EH15: Port 5H 23
Magdalene Pl. EH15: Port 5H 23
Maidencraig Ct. EH4: Edin 1A 20
Maidencraig Cres. EH4: Edin 1A 20
Maidencraig Gro. EH4: Edin 1A 20
Maid of the Forth (Boat Trips) 1J 7
Main Point EH3: Edin 6C 4
Mains Gdns. EH33: Tran 1H 27
Mains of Craigmillar
EH16: Edin 2D 34
Main St. EH4: Edin 7C 10
EH14: Bal 3E 36
EH20: Loan 6K 39
EH22: Newt 7C 42
EH23: Gore 7E 48
EH25: Rosl 3A 46
EH28: Rat 2D 28
EH29: Kltn 1A 16
EH30: Dalm 3K 7
EH33: Elph 7F 27
EH52: Winch 7A 6
Maitland Av. EH21: Muss 2C 24
Maitland Hog La.
EH29: Kltn 2A 16
Maitland Pk. Rd.
EH21: Muss 2C 24
Maitland Rd. EH29: Kltn 1A 16
Maitland St. EH21: Muss 2C 24
Malbet Pk. EH16: Edin 5B 34
Malbet Wynd EH16: Edin 5B 34
Malcolm Ho. EH4: Edin 6J 11
Mall Av. EH21: Muss 2E 24
Malleny Av. EH14: Bal 4E 36
Malleny Garden 3F 37
Malleny Millgate EH14: Bal 6F 37
MALLENY MILLS 5F 37
Malleny Pk. 3F 37
Malta Grn. EH4: Edin 1F 21
Malta Ter. EH4: Edin 1F 21
Manderston Ct. EH6: Edin 6F 13
Manderston St. EH6: Edin 6E 12
Mannering Pl. EH16: Edin 4B 34
Manor Pl. EH3: Edin 3E 20
Manse La. EH21: Muss 2F 25
EH32: Port S 3G 15
Manse Rd. EH12: Edin 5F 19
EH25: Rosl 3A 46
EH29: Kltn 2A 16
Manse St. EH12: Edin 5F 19
Mansfield Av. EH21: Muss 3E 24
EH22: Newt 7D 42
Mansfield Ct. EH21: Muss 3F 25
Mansfield Pl. EH3: Edin 1H 21
EH21: Muss 3E 24
EH22: Newt 7D 42
Mansfield Rd. EH14: Bal 4E 36
EH21: Muss 2E 24
EH22: Newt 7D 42
Mansionhouse Rd.
EH9: Edin 6H 21
Marchbank Dr. EH14: Bal 5E 36
Marchbank Gdns. EH14: Bal 5E 36
Marchbank Gro. EH14: Bal 5E 36
Marchbank Pl. EH14: Bal 5E 36
Marchbank Way EH14: Bal 4E 36
Marchburn Dr. EH26: Pen 2A 50
Marchfield Gro. EH4: Edin 7D 10
Marchfield Pk. EH4: Edin 7C 10
Marchfield Pk. La. EH4: Edin 7C 10
Marchfield Ter. EH4: Edin 1J 19
March Gait EH4: Edin 1H 19
March Gro. EH4: Edin 1H 19
Marchhall Cres. EH16: Edin 6A 22
Marchhall Pl. EH16: Edin 6K 21
Marchhall Rd. EH16: Edin 6A 22
MARCHMONT 6H 21
Marchmont Cres. EH9: Edin 6H 21
(not continuous)
Marchmont Rd. EH9: Edin 6G 21
Marchmont St. EH9: Edin 6G 21
March Pines EH4: Edin 1H 19
March Rd. EH4: Edin 1H 19
Marchwood Ct. EH33: Elph 7F 27
Marco's Leisure Cen. 4E 20 (7A 4)
Mardale Cres. EH10: Edin 7E 20
Margaret Rose Cres.
EH10: Edin 7G 33
Margaret Rose Dr.
EH10: Edin 7G 33
Margaret Rose Loan
EH10: Edin 7G 33
Margaret Rose Wlk.
EH10: Edin 7G 33
Margaret Rose Way
EH10: Edin 7G 33
Marine Dr. EH4: Edin 4A 10
Marine Esplanade EH6: Leith 4H 13
Marionville Av. EH7: Edin 1B 22
Marionville Cres. EH7: Edin 1C 22
Marionville Dr. EH7: Edin 1C 22
Marionville Gro. EH7: Edin 1C 22
Marionville Medway
EH7: Edin 1C 22
Marionville Pk. EH7: Edin 1B 22
Marionville Rd. EH7: Edin 2A 22
Marischal Pl. EH4: Edin 2A 20
Maritime La. EH6: Leith 5F 13
Maritime St. EH6: Leith 5F 13
Market Loan EH33: Tran 1G 27
Market Pl. EH22: Dalk 2C 42
Market St. EH1: Edin 3H 21 (4E 4)
EH21: Muss 2D 24
Market Vw. EH33: Tran 1G 27
Market Way EH33: Tran 1G 27
Marlborough St. EH15: Port 3H 23
Marmion Av. EH25: Rosl 2K 45
Marmion Cres. EH16: Edin 2B 34
Marshall Pl. EH4: Edin 7C 10
Marshall Rd. EH29: Kltn 2A 16
Marshall's Ct.
EH1: Edin 2J 21 (1G 5)
Marshall St. EH8: Edin 4H 21 (6F 5)
EH32: Cock 3F 15
Martello Ct. EH4: Edin 5D 10
Martin Gro. EH19: Bonn 5K 41
Martin Pl. EH22: Dalk 3A 42
Maryburn Rd. EH22: East 5E 42
Maryfield EH7: Edin 1K 21 (1K 5)
EH15: Port 2H 23
Maryfield Pl.
EH7: Edin 1A 22 (1K 5)
EH19: Bonn 6J 41
Mary's Pl. *EH4: Edin 1E 20*
(off Raeburn Pl.)
Mary Tree Ho. EH17: Edin 4D 34
Masefield Way EH12: Edin A 2H 17
Mason Pl. EH18: Las 7F 41
Matthew Architecture Gallery, The
5E 4
Matthews Dr. EH22: Newt 1B 48
Maulsford Av. EH22: Dan 5H 35
Maurice Pl. EH9: Edin 2H 33
MAURICEWOOD 7D 44
Mauricewood Av. EH26: Pen 7D 44
Mauricewood Bank
EH26: Pen 7D 44
Mauricewood Gro. EH26: Pen 7D 44
Mauricewood Pk. EH26: Pen 7D 44
Mauricewood Ri. EH26: Pen 7D 44
Mauricewood Rd. EH26: Pen 5C 44
Mavisbank EH20: Loan 6C 40
Mavisbank Pl. EH18: Las 7E 40
Maxton Ct. EH22: Dalk 2C 42
Maxwell St. EH10: Edin 1E 32
Maybank Vs. EH12: Edin 4F 19
Mayburn Av. EH20: Loan 5B 40
Mayburn Bank EH20: Loan 5B 40
Mayburn Cl. EH20: Loan 4B 40
Mayburn Ct. EH20: Loan 5B 40
Mayburn Cres. EH20: Loan 4B 40
Mayburn Dr. EH20: Loan 5B 40
Mayburn Gdns. EH20: Loan 4B 40
Mayburn Gro. EH20: Loan 5B 40
Mayburn Hill EH20: Loan 5B 40
Mayburn Loan EH20: Loan 4B 40
Mayburn Ter. EH20: Loan 4B 40
Mayburn Va. EH20: Loan 5A 40
Mayburn Wlk. EH20: Loan 5B 40
Maybury Dr. EH12: Edin 3C 18
Maybury Junc. 5C 18
Maybury Rd. EH4: Edin 5C 18
EH12: Edin 5C 18
May Ct. EH4: Edin 5D 10
MAYFIELD
Dalkeith 6F 43
Edinburgh 7K 21
Mayfield Av. EH21: Muss 5D 24
Mayfield Ct. EH20: Loan 6C 40
Mayfield Cres. EH20: Loan 6C 40
EH21: Muss 4C 24
Mayfield Gdns. EH9: Edin 7K 21
Mayfield Gdns. La. EH9: Edin 7K 21
Mayfield Ind. Est. EH22: May 1E 48
EH22: Newt 7E 42
Mayfield Leisure Cen. 6F 43
Mayfield Pk. EH21: Muss 5D 24
Mayfield Pl. EH12: Edin 5F 19
EH21: Muss 5D 24
EH22: May 7F 43
Mayfield Rd. EH9: Edin 7K 21
EH22: East 5F 43
Mayfield Ter. EH9: Edin 7K 21
MAYSHADE 5K 41
Mayshade Rd. EH20: Loan 4B 40
Mayville Bank EH21: Muss 2J 25
Mayville Gdns. EH5: Edin 4B 12
Mayville Gdns. E. EH5: Edin 4B 12
MEADOWBANK 2C 22
Meadowbank EH8: Edin 2B 22
Meadowbank Av. EH8: Edin 2B 22
Meadowbank Cres. EH8: Edin 2B 22
Meadowbank Pl. EH8: Edin 2B 22
Meadowbank Shop. Pk.
EH7: Edin 1A 22
Meadowbank Sports Cen. 2B 22
Meadowbank Stadium 2B 22
Meadowbank Ter. EH8: Edin 2B 22
MEADOWFIELD 4D 22
Meadowfield Av. EH8: Edin 4D 22
Meadowfield Ct. EH8: Edin 4D 22
Meadowfield Dr. EH8: Edin 4D 22
Meadowfield Gdns.
EH8: Edin 5D 22
Meadowfield Rd. EH12: Edin 3A 18
Meadowfield Ter. EH8: Edin 5D 22
Meadowhouse Ct. EH12: Edin 5G 19
Meadowhouse Rd.
EH12: Edin 5G 19
Meadow La. EH8: Edin 5H 21 (7F 5)
MEADOWMILL 7F 15
Meadowmill Loan EH33: Tran 1H 27
Meadowmill Sports Cen. 7F 15
Meadow Pl. EH9: Edin 5G 21
EH25: Bil 7J 39
Meadow Pl. La. *EH9: Edin 6H 21*
(off Roseneath Ter.)
Meadow Pl. Rd. EH12: Edin 5E 18
Meadow Rd. EH14: Cur 5B 30
Meadowside EH33: Tran 3J 27
Meadowspot EH10: Edin 2C 32
Mearenside EH12: Edin 3C 18
Medwin Ho. EH11: Edin 3E 30
Meeting Ho. Dr. EH33: Tran 2G 27
Megabowl
Dalry 5E 20
Fort Kinnaird 7J 23

70 A-Z Edinburgh

Meggat Pl.—Murrays, The

Meggat Pl. EH26: Pen .7E **44**
Meggetgate EH14: Edin .1A **32**
Meggetland .1B **32**
Meggetland Ter. EH14: Edin .1C **32**
Melgund Ter. EH7: Edin .1H **21**
Melville Cres. EH3: Edin .3E **20**
Melville Dr. EH9: Edin .5G **21** (7C **4**)
Melville Dykes Rd.
EH18: Las .4H **41**
EH22: Dalk .3K **41**
Melville Ga. EH22: Dalk .2K **41**
Melville Ga. Rd. EH22: Dalk .2K **41**
Melville Grange Cotts.
EH18: Las .1H **41**
Melville Pl. EH2: Edin .3A **4**
Melville Rd. EH22: Dalk .3A **42**
Melville Monument .2H **21** (2E **4**)
Melville St. EH3: Edin .3E **20** (4A **4**)
Melville St. La. EH3: Edin .3E **20**
EH15: Port .3H **23**
Melville Ter. EH9: Edin .6H **21**
EH22: Dalk .4A **42**
Melville Vw. EH18: Las .5G **41**
Mentone Av. EH15: Port .2H **23**
Mentone Gdns. EH9: Edin .7K **21**
Mentone Ter. EH9: Edin .1K **33**
Mercat Cross .4F **5**
Merchant St. EH1: Edin .5E **4**
MERCHISTON .7D **20**
Merchiston Av. EH10: Edin .6E **20**
Merchiston Bank Av.
EH10: Edin .7E **20**
Merchiston Bank Gdns.
EH10: Edin .7E **20**
Merchiston Cres. EH10: Edin .7E **20**
Merchiston Gdns. EH10: Edin .1D **32**
Merchiston Gro. EH11: Edin .7C **20**
Merchiston M. EH10: Edin .6E **20**
Merchiston Pk. EH10: Edin .6E **20**
Merchiston Pl. EH10: Edin .6E **20**
Merlyon Way EH26: Pen .7B **44**
Mertoun Pl. EH11: Edin .6D **20**
Methven Ter. EH18: Las .7F **41**
Meuse La. EH2: Edin .3H **21** (3E **4**)
Middleby St. EH9: Edin .7K **21**
Middlefield EH7: Edin .7D **12**
Middleknowe EH14: Edin .4E **30**
Middle Mdw. Wlk.
EH3: Edin .5H **21** (7E **4**)
Middlepark EH14: Edin .4E **30**
Middleshot EH14: Edin .4E **30**
Middleshot Sq. EH32: Pres .5F **15**
Midfield Ho. EH18: Las .1E **46**
Mid Gillsland Rd. EH10: Edin .7D **20**
Mid Gogarloch Syke
EH12: Edin .6C **18**
Mid Liberton EH16: Edin .2A **34**
Midlothian Indoor Bowling Club
.2B **42**
Midlothian Ski Cen. .3E **38**
Midmar Av. EH10: Edin .2G **33**
Midmar Dr. EH10: Edin .3G **33**
Midmar Gdns. EH10: Edin .2F **33**
Mid New Cultins EH11: Edin .2D **30**
Mid Rd. EH32: Pres .7D **14**
Mid Rd. Ind. Est EH32: Pres .7D **14**
Mid Steil EH10: Edin .3C **32**
Mid Ter. EH30: S Q'fry .1H **7**
MILESTONE HOUSE (HOSPICE)
.4C **32**
Millar Cres. EH10: Edin .1E **32**
Millar Pl. EH10: Edin .1E **32**
Millar Pl. La. EH10: Edin .1E **32**
[illegible]
Millbank EH14: Bal .4E **36**
Millbank Gro. EH23: Gore .7E **48**
Millbrae Wynd *EH14: Edin* .*2K **31***
(off Inglis Grn. Rd.)
Miller Ct. EH33: Tran .3F **27**
Millerfield Pl. EH9: Edin .6H **21**
Millerhill Rd. EH22: Dalk .2H **35**
Miller Row EH4: Edin .3E **20**
Millhill EH21: Muss .2F **25**
Millhill Cotts. EH22: Newt .6C **42**
Millhill La. EH21: Muss .2F **25**
Millhill Wynd EH21: Muss .2F **25**
Mill La. EH6: Leith .5E **12**
Millstone Brow Cotts.
EH23: Gore .7G **49**
Mill Wynd EH32: Pres .5D **14**
Milnacre EH6: Edin .5C **12**
Milne's Ct. EH1: Edin .4D **4**
Milrig Cotts. EH29: Kltn .3A **16**
MILTON BRIDGE .4F **45**
Milton Cres. EH15: Port .5G **23**
Milton Dr. EH15: Port .4K **23**
Milton Gdns. Nth. EH15: Port .5G **23**
Milton Gdns. Sth. EH15: Port .5G **23**
Milton Gro. EH15: Port .1A **24**
Milton Link EH15: Port .5J **23**
Milton Rd. EH15: Port .5G **23**
Milton Rd. E. EH15: Port .5J **23**
Milton Rd. W. EH15: Edin .5E **22**
Milton St. EH8: Edin .2A **22**
Milton Ter. EH15: Port .1A **24**
Miner's Ter. EH21: Wall .3K **25**
Minstrel Ct. EH25: Rosl .3A **46**
Minto St. EH9: Edin .6K **21**
Mitchell St. EH6: Leith .5F **13**
EH22: Dalk .2B **42**
Mitchell Way EH33: Tran .1H **27**
Moat Dr. EH14: Edin .7B **20**
Moat Ho. EH14: Edin .7B **20**
Moat Pl. EH14: Edin .7B **20**
Moat St. EH14: Edin .7B **20**
Moat Ter. EH14: Edin .7B **20**
Moat Vw. EH25: Rosl .3K **45**
Moffat Av. EH19: Bonn .7H **41**
Moira Pk. EH7: Edin .2E **22**
Moira Ter. EH7: Edin .2E **22**
(not continuous)
Moira Ter. La. EH7: Edin .2E **22**
Moir Av. EH21: Muss .2J **25**
Moir Cres. EH21: Muss .2J **25**
Moir Dr. EH21: Muss .2K **25**
Moir Pl. EH21: Muss .2J **25**
Moir Ter. EH21: Muss .2J **25**
Moncrieffe Ho. EH17: Edin .4D **34**
Moncrieff Ter. EH9: Edin .6J **21**
Monkbarns Gdns. EH16: Edin .4B **34**
Monksrig Rd. EH26: Pen .2A **50**
MONKSWOOD .2D **48**
Monkswood Rd. EH22: Newt .2D **48**
MONKTONHALL .5D **24**
Monktonhall Pl. EH21: Muss .5D **24**
Monktonhall Ter. EH21: Muss .4D **24**
Monkwood Ct. EH9: Edin .7H **21**
Monmouth Ter. EH3: Edin .5A **12**
Montague St.
EH8: Edin .5J **21** (7H **5**)
Montagu Ter. EH3: Edin .6A **12**
Montgomery St.
EH7: Edin .1J **21** (1K **5**)
Montgomery St. La.
EH7: Edin .1J **21** (1G **5**)
Montpelier EH10: Edin .6F **20**
Montpelier Pk. EH10: Edin .6E **20**
Montpelier Ter. EH10: Edin .6E **20**
Montrose Ter.
EH7: Edin .2K **21** (1K **5**)
Moorfield Cotts. EH22: Dalk .4J **35**
Moorfoot Ct. EH19: Bonn .6H **41**
Moorfoot Pl. EH19: Bonn .7H **41**
EH26: Pen .1C **50**
Moorfoot Vw. EH19: Bonn .7H **41**
EH23: Gore .7E **48**
EH25: Bil .1J **45**
Moray Pk. EH7: Edin .1A **22**
Moray Pk. Ter. EH7: Edin .2A **22**
Moray Pl. EH3: Edin .2F **21** (2A **4**)
MOREDUN .5E **34**
Moredun Dykes Rd.
EH17: Edin .7D **34**
Moredun Ho. EH4: Edin .7J **11**
EH17: Edin .4D **34**
Moredun Pk. Ct. EH17: Edin .5D **34**
Moredun Pk. Dr. EH17: Edin .5D **34**
Moredun Pk. Gdns.
EH17: Edin .4D **34**
Moredun Pk. Grn. EH17: Edin .5E **34**
Moredun Pk. Gro. EH17: Edin .5E **34**
Moredun Pk. Loan
EH17: Edin .5D **34**
Moredun Pk. Rd. EH17: Edin .5D **34**
Moredun Pk. St. EH17: Edin .5D **34**
Moredun Pk. Vw. EH17: Edin .5D **34**
Moredun Pk. Wlk. EH17: Edin .5E **34**
Moredun Pk. Way EH17: Edin .5D **34**
Moredunvale Bank
EH17: Edin .4D **34**
Moredunvale Grn. EH17: Edin .4D **34**
Moredunvale Gro. EH17: Edin .4D **34**
Moredunvale Loan
EH17: Edin .4D **34**
Moredunvale Pk. EH17: Edin .4D **34**
Moredunvale Pl. EH17: Edin .4D **34**
Moredunvale Rd. EH17: Edin .4C **34**
Moredunvale Vw. EH17: Edin .4D **34**
Moredunvale Way
EH17: Edin .4D **34**
Morham Gait EH10: Edin .4C **32**
Morham Gdns. EH10: Edin .4C **32**
Morham Lea EH10: Edin .4C **32**
Morham Pk. EH10: Edin .4C **32**
Morison Gdns. EH30: S Q'fry .1G **7**
MORNINGSIDE .2D **32**
Morningside Ct. EH10: Edin .2E **32**
Morningside Dr. EH10: Edin .2D **32**
Morningside Gdns.
EH10: Edin .2D **32**
Morningside Gro. EH10: Edin .2D **32**
Morningside Pk. EH10: Edin .1E **32**
Morningside Pl. EH10: Edin .1E **32**
Morningside Rd. EH10: Edin .7E **20**
Morningside Ter. EH10: Edin .1E **32**
Morrison Av. EH33: Tran .3J **27**
Morrison Cir. *EH3: Edin* .*4E **20***
(off Morrison Cres.)
Morrison Cres. EH3: Edin .4E **20**
Morrison Link EH3: Edin .4E **20**
Morrison's Cl. EH1: Edin .4G **5**
Morrison's Haven EH32: Pres .7A **14**
Morrison St. EH3: Edin .4E **20** (6A **4**)
Morris Rd. EH22: Newt .7E **42**
MORTONHALL .6G **33**
Mortonhall Crematorium
EH16: Edin .7K **33**
Mortonhall Ga. EH16: Edin .7H **33**
Mortonhall Pk. Av.
EH17: Edin .7K **33**
Mortonhall Pk. Bank
EH17: Edin .7A **34**
Mortonhall Pk. Cres.
EH17: Edin .7A **34**
Mortonhall Pk. Dr.
EH17: Edin .7A **34**
Mortonhall Pk. Gdns.
EH17: Edin .7K **33**
Mortonhall Pk. Grn.
EH17: Edin .7A **34**
Mortonhall Pk. Gro.
EH17: Edin .7K **33**
Mortonhall Pk. Loan
EH17: Edin .7K **33**
Mortonhall Pk. Pl.
EH17: Edin .7A **34**
Mortonhall Pk. Ter.
EH17: Edin .7A **34**
Mortonhall Pk. Vw.
EH17: Edin .7K **33**
Mortonhall Pk. Way
EH17: Edin .7K **33**
Mortonhall Rd. EH9: Edin .1H **33**
Morton Mains Cotts.
EH10: Edin .1G **39**
Morton St. EH15: Port .4J **23**
(not continuous)
Morton St. Sth. EH15: Port .4J **23**
Morvenside EH14: Edin .4E **30**
Morvenside Cl. EH14: Edin .4E **30**
Morven St. EH4: Edin .2E **18**
Mossend Cotts. EH23: Gore .6G **49**
Mossgiel Wlk. EH16: Edin .3A **34**
Moston Ter. EH9: Edin .7K **21**
Moubray Gro. EH30: S Q'fry .2H **7**
Mound, The EH1: Edin .3G **21** (3D **4**)
EH2: Edin .3G **21** (3D **4**)
Mound Pl. EH1: Edin .3G **21** (4D **4**)
Mt. Alvernia EH16: Edin .5B **34**
MOUNTCASTLE .3F **23**
Mountcastle Bank EH8: Edin .3F **23**
Mountcastle Cres. EH8: Edin .3E **22**
Mountcastle Dr. Nth.
EH8: Edin .3E **22**
Mountcastle Dr. Sth.
EH15: Edin, Port .4F **23**
Mountcastle Gdns. EH8: Edin .3E **22**
Mountcastle Grn. EH8: Edin .2E **22**
Mountcastle Gro. EH8: Edin .3E **22**
Mountcastle Loan EH8: Edin .3E **22**
Mountcastle Pk. EH8: Edin .2E **22**
Mountcastle Pl. EH8: Edin .2E **22**
Mountcastle Ter. EH8: Edin .3E **22**
Mt. Grange EH9: Edin .7G **21**
Mounthooly Loan EH10: Edin .7G **33**
Mountjoy Ct. EH21: Muss .1E **24**
Mountjoy Ter. EH21: Muss .1E **24**
Mt. Lodge Pl. EH15: Port .3H **23**
Mt. Vernon Rd. EH16: Edin .4B **34**
Mucklets Av. EH21: Muss .4C **24**
Mucklets Ct. EH21: Muss .4C **24**
Mucklets Cres. EH21: Muss .4C **24**
Mucklets Dr. EH21: Muss .4C **24**
Mucklets Pl. EH21: Muss .4C **24**
Mucklets Rd. EH21: Muss .5B **24**
Muirdale Ter. EH4: Edin .1K **19**
Muirend Av. EH14: J Grn .5G **31**
Muirfield Gdns. EH20: Loan .6C **40**
Muir Hall EH3: Edin .3E **20**
Muirhead Pl. EH26: Pen .6D **44**
MUIRHOUSE .5D **10**
Muirhouse Av. EH4: Edin .6E **10**
Muirhouse Av. Nth.
EH4: Edin .5E **10**
Muirhouse Bank EH4: Edin .6E **10**
Muirhouse Cl. EH4: Edin .6D **10**
Muirhouse Ct. EH4: Edin .5D **10**
Muirhouse Cres. EH4: Edin .5E **10**
Muirhouse Dr. EH4: Edin .5D **10**
Muirhouse Gdns. EH4: Edin .5D **10**
Muirhouse Grn. EH4: Edin .6D **10**
Muirhouse Gro. EH4: Edin .5D **10**
Muirhouse Loan EH4: Edin .5E **10**
Muirhouse Medway
EH4: Edin .6D **10**
Muirhouse Pk. EH4: Edin .6D **10**
Muirhouse Parkway
EH4: Edin .5D **10**
Muirhouse Pl. E. EH4: Edin .6E **10**
Muirhouse Pl. W. EH4: Edin .6E **10**
Muirhouse Ter. EH4: Edin .6D **10**
Muirhouse Vw. EH4: Edin .5D **10**
Muirhouse Way EH4: Edin .6E **10**
Muirpark EH22: Dalk .4A **42**
Muirpark Ct. EH33: Tran .3J **27**
Muirpark Dr. EH33: Tran .3J **27**
Muirpark Gdns. EH33: Tran .3J **27**
Muirpark Gro. EH33: Tran .3J **27**
Muirpark Pl. EH33: Tran .3J **27**
Muirpark Rd. EH33: Tran .3J **27**
Muirpark Ter. EH33: Tran .3J **27**
Muirpark Wynd EH33: Tran .3J **27**
Muirside EH10: Edin .7C **32**
Muirside Dr. EH33: Tran .3G **27**
Muir Wood Cres. EH14: Cur .7D **30**
Muir Wood Dr. EH14: Cur .7D **30**
Muir Wood Gro. EH14: Cur .7D **30**
Muir Wood Pl. EH14: Cur .7D **30**
Muir Wood Rd. EH14: Cur .7C **30**
Mulberry Pl. EH6: Edin .5C **12**
Multrees Wlk. EH1: Edin .2E **4**
Munro Dr. EH13: Edin .7J **31**
Munro Pl. EH3: Edin .7B **12**
Murano Pl. EH7: Edin .1K **21**
Murderdean Rd. EH22: Newt .7B **42**
Murdoch Ter. EH11: Edin .5E **20**
Murieston Cres. EH11: Edin .5C **20**
Murieston Cres. La.
EH11: Edin .5C **20**
Murieston La. EH11: Edin .5C **20**
Murieston Pl. EH11: Edin .5C **20**
Murieston Rd. EH11: Edin .5C **20**
Murieston Ter. EH11: Edin .5C **20**
Murrayburn App. EH14: Edin .3F **31**
Murrayburn Dr. EH14: Edin .3E **30**
Murrayburn Gdns.
EH14: Edin .3F **31**
Murrayburn Ga. EH14: Edin .4F **31**
Murrayburn Grn. EH14: Edin [illegible]
Murrayburn Gro. EH14: Edin .3G **31**
Murrayburn Pk. EH14: Edin .3F **31**
Murrayburn Pl. EH14: Edin .3F **31**
Murrayburn Rd. EH14: Edin .3F **31**
Murray Cotts. EH12: Edin .5E **18**
MURRAYFIELD .4A **20**
Murrayfield .5A **20**
Murrayfield Av. EH12: Edin .4B **20**
MURRAYFIELD BUPA HOSPITAL
.4J **19**
Murrayfield Dr. EH12: Edin .4A **20**
Murrayfield Gdns.
EH12: Edin .4B **20**
Murrayfield Ice Rink .5A **20**
Murrayfield Pl. EH12: Edin .4B **20**
Murrayfield Rd. EH12: Edin .3A **20**
Murrayfield Wanderers FC .5A **20**
Murray Pl. EH12: Edin .5G **19**
Murrays, The EH17: Edin .1C **40**

Oak Av.—Pilrig Cotts.

O

Oak Av. EH20: Loan .6K **39**
Oak Cres. EH22: May .7G **43**
Oakfield Pl. EH8: Edin .4J **21** (5H **5**)
Oak La. EH12: Edin .2G **19**
Oaklea Cotts. EH23: Gore .6G **49**
Oak Pl. EH22: May .6G **43**
Oakville Ter. EH6: Edin .6G **13**
Observatory Grn. EH9: Edin .2J **33**
Observatory Rd. EH9: Edin .2H **33**
Ocean Dr. EH6: Leith .4D **12**
Ocean Terminal EH6: Leith .3D **12**
Ochil Ct. EH30: S Q'fry .2H **7**
Ochiltree Gdns. EH16: Edin .3C **34**
Odeon Cinema
Edinburgh .4F 21 (6B 4)
Wester Hailes .4F 31
Ogilvie Ter. EH11: Edin .7C **20**
Old Assembly Cl. EH1: Edin .4F **5**
Old Broughton
EH3: Edin .1H **21** (1E **4**)
Old Burdiehouse Rd.
EH17: Edin .2A **40**
Old Church La. EH15: Edin .5C **22**
OLD CRAIGHALL .7C 24
OLD CRAIGHALL JUNC. .6D 24
Old Craighall Rd.
EH21: Muss .7C **24**
EH22: Dalk .5K **35** & 7D **24**
Old Dalkeith Rd. EH16: Edin .1B **34**
EH22: Dalk .1K **41**
EH22: Dan .5G **35**
Old Edinburgh Rd.
EH22: Dalk .2B **42**
Old Farm Av. EH13: Edin .5K **31**
Old Farm Ct. EH13: Edin .5K **31**
Old Farm Pl. EH13: Edin .6K **31**
Old Fishmarket Cl.
EH1: Edin .3H **21** (4F **5**)
Old Kirk Rd. EH12: Edin .4G **19**
Old Liston Rd. EH28: Nbdge .5A **16**
Old Mill La. EH16: Edin .2A **34**
Old Newmills Rd. EH14: Bal .2F **37**
OLD PENTLAND .4J 39
Old Pentland Rd. EH10: Edin .5H **39**
Old Playhouse Cl.
EH8: Edin .3J **21** (4H **5**)
Old Star Rd. EH22: Newt .1B **48**
Old Tolbooth Wynd
EH8: Edin .3J **21** (3H **5**)
OLD TOWN .4H 21 (5E 4)
Oliphant Gdns. EH21: Wall .3K **25**
Olivebank Retail Pk.
EH21: Muss .2C **24**
Olive Bank Rd. EH21: Muss .2C **24**
Omni Cen. EH1: Edin .2J **21** (1G **5**)
Open Eye Gallery .1D 4
Orchard, The *EH21: Muss .3D 24*
(off Stoneyhill Farm Rd.)
EH33: Tran .1G **27**
Orchard Bank EH4: Edin .2C **20**
Orchard Brae EH4: Edin .1D **20**
Orchard Brae Av. EH4: Edin .2C **20**
Orchard Brae Gdns.
EH4: Edin .2C **20**
Orchard Brae Gdns. W.
EH4: Edin .2C **20**
Orchard Brae W. EH4: Edin .1D **20**
Orchard Cres. EH4: Edin .2B **20**
EH32: Pres .6D **14**
Orchard Dr. EH4: Edin .2B **20**
Orchardfield Av. EH12: Edin .5F **19**
Orchardfield La. EH6: Edin .7E **12**
Orchardfield Ter. EH27: Wilk .7A **28**
Orchard Gro. EH4: Edin .2D **20**
Orchardhead Loan
EH16: Edin .4A **34**
Orchardhead Rd. EH16: Edin .3A **34**
Orchard Pk. EH33: Tran .1G **27**
Orchard Pl. EH4: Edin .1C **20**
Orchard Rd. EH4: Edin .2C **20**
Orchard Rd. Sth. EH4: Edin .2B **20**
Orchard Ter. EH4: Edin .2C **20**
Orchard Toll EH4: Edin .2C **20**
Orchard Vw. EH22: Dalk .3A **42**
Ormelie Ter. EH15: Port .3J **23**
Ormidale Ter. EH12: Edin .4A **20**
Ormiston Av. EH33: Tran .2J **27**
Ormiston Cres. E. EH33: Tran .2J **27**
Ormiston Cres. W. EH33: Tran .2J **27**
Ormiston Pl. EH32: Pres .6C **14**
Ormiston Rd. EH33: Tran .2H **27**
Ormiston Ter. EH12: Edin .5F **19**
Orrok Pk. EH16: Edin .2A **34**
Orwell Pl. EH11: Edin .5D **20**
Orwell Ter. EH11: Edin .5D **20**
Osborne Ct. EH32: Cock .3G **15**
Osborne Ter. EH12: Edin .4D **20**
EH32: Cock, Port S .3G **15**
Oswald Ct. EH9: Edin .1H **33**
Oswald Rd. EH9: Edin .1H **33**
Oswald Ter. EH12: Edin .5F **19**
EH32: Pres .6E **14**
Otterburn Pk. EH14: Edin .4K **31**
Our Dynamic Earth .3K 21 (4J 5)
Oxcars Ct. EH4: Edin .5D **10**
Oxcraig St. EH5: Edin .3J **11**
Oxford St. EH8: Edin .5K **21**
Oxford Ter. EH4: Edin .2E **20**
Oxgangs Av. EH13: Edin .6C **32**
Oxgangs Bank EH13: Edin .6D **32**
Oxgangs Brae EH13: Edin .6D **32**
Oxgangs B'way. *EH13: Edin .6D 32*
(off Oxgangs Bank)
Oxgangs Cres. EH13: Edin .5D **32**
Oxgangs Dr. EH13: Edin .5C **32**
(not continuous)
Oxgangs Farm Av.
EH13: Edin .6C **32**
Oxgangs Farm Dr.
EH13: Edin .6C **32**
Oxgangs Farm Gdns.
EH13: Edin .6C **32**
Oxgangs Farm Gro.
EH13: Edin .6C **32**
Oxgangs Farm Loan
EH13: Edin .6C **32**
Oxgangs Farm Ter.
EH13: Edin .6C **32**
Oxgangs Gdns. EH13: Edin .5C **32**
Oxgangs Grn. EH13: Edin .5D **32**
Oxgangs Gro. EH13: Edin .5D **32**
Oxgangs Hill EH13: Edin .5D **32**
Oxgangs Ho. EH13: Edin .5C **32**
Oxgangs Loan EH13: Edin .5D **32**
Oxgangs Medway EH13: Edin .6D **32**
Oxgangs Pk. EH13: Edin .6D **32**
Oxgangs Path EH13: Edin .6D **32**
Oxgangs Path E. *EH13: Edin .6D 32*
(off Oxgangs Brae)
Oxgangs Pl. EH13: Edin .5C **32**
Oxgangs Ri. EH13: Edin .5D **32**
Oxgangs Rd. EH10: Edin .7D **32**
EH13: Edin .7D **32**
Oxgangs Rd. Nth.
EH13: Edin .4B **32**
EH14: Edin .4B **32**
Oxgangs Row EH13: Edin .6D **32**
Oxgangs St. EH13: Edin .6D **32**
Oxgangs Ter. EH13: Edin .6C **32**
Oxgangs Vw. EH13: Edin .6D **32**
Ox Wlk. EH32: Pres .6C **14**

P

Paddock, The EH21: Muss .1F **25**
Paddockholm, The
EH12: Edin .5G **19**
Paisley Av. EH8: Edin .3D **22**
Paisley Cl. EH1: Edin .4G **5**
Paisley Cres. EH8: Edin .3C **22**
Paisley Dr. EH8: Edin .4D **22**
Paisley Gdns. EH8: Edin .3C **22**
Paisley Gro. EH8: Edin .4D **22**
Paisley Ter. EH8: Edin .3C **22**
Palace of Holyroodhouse
.3K 21 (3K 5)
Palmer Pl. EH14: Cur .1H **37**
Palmer Rd. EH14: Cur .7B **30**
Palmerston Pl. EH12: Edin .3D **20**
Palmerston Pl. La.
EH12: Edin .4E **20**
Palmerston Rd. EH9: Edin .6H **21**
Pandore Wlk. EH32: Pres .6C **14**
Pankhurst Loan EH22: Dalk .2F **43**
Panmure Cl. EH8: Edin .3H **5**
Panmure Pl.
EH3: Edin .5G **21** (7C **4**)
Pansey Wlk. EH11: Edin .6A **20**
Pape's Cotts. EH12: Edin .4B **20**
Paradykes Av. EH20: Loan .5A **40**
Park Av. EH15: Port .4G **23**
EH20: Loan .6A **40**
EH21: Muss .3G **25**
EH23: Gore .5E **48**
EH25: Bil .7H **39**
Park Ct. EH21: Muss .3G **25**
Park Cres. EH16: Edin .4B **34**
EH19: Bonn .6H **41**
EH20: Loan .6B **40**
EH22: East .5E **42**
Parker Av. EH7: Edin .2E **22**
Parker Rd. EH7: Edin .2E **22**
Parker Ter. EH7: Edin .2F **23**
Park Gdns. EH16: Edin .4B **34**
EH21: Muss .3F **25**
Park Gro. EH16: Edin .5B **34**
Parkgrove Av. EH4: Edin .1E **18**
Parkgrove Bank EH4: Edin .1E **18**
Parkgrove Cres. EH4: Edin .1E **18**
Parkgrove Dr. EH4: Edin .1D **18**
Parkgrove Gdns. EH4: Edin .1E **18**
Parkgrove Grn. EH4: Edin .1E **18**
Parkgrove Loan EH4: Edin .1E **18**
Parkgrove Neuk EH4: Edin .1E **18**
Parkgrove Path EH4: Edin .1F **19**
Park Gro. Pl. EH21: Muss .3G **25**
Parkgrove Pl. EH4: Edin .1E **18**
Parkgrove Rd. EH4: Edin .1E **18**
Parkgrove Row EH4: Edin .1E **18**
Parkgrove St. EH4: Edin .1F **19**
Park Gro. Ter. EH21: Muss .3G **25**
Parkgrove Ter. EH4: Edin .1E **18**
Parkgrove Vw. EH4: Edin .1E **18**
PARKHEAD .2G 31
Parkhead Av. EH11: Edin .2G **31**
Parkhead Cres. EH11: Edin .2G **31**
Parkhead Dr. EH11: Edin .2G **31**
Parkhead Gdns. EH11: Edin .2G **31**
Parkhead Gro. EH11: Edin .2G **31**
Parkhead Loan EH11: Edin .2H **31**
Parkhead Pk. EH22: East .5E **42**
Parkhead Pl. EH11: Edin .2G **31**
EH22: East .5E **42**
Parkhead St. EH11: Edin .2G **31**
Parkhead Ter. EH11: Edin .2H **31**
Parkhead Vw. EH11: Edin .2G **31**
Parkhill EH23: Gore .5D **48**
Park La. EH15: Edin .4G **23**
EH21: Muss .3G **25**
Park Pl. EH6: Newh .4B **12**
Park Rd. EH6: Newh .4B **12**
EH19: Bonn .6H **41**
EH22: Dalk .3B **42**
EH22: Newt .7D **42**
EH23: Gore .5E **48**
EH32: Port S .3H **15**
Parkside EH28: Nbdge .5A **16**
Parkside Ct. EH22: Dalk .3B **42**
Parkside Pl. EH22: Dalk .2C **42**
Parkside St. EH8: Edin .5K **21** (7J **5**)
Parkside Ter.
EH16: Edin .5K **21** (7J **5**)
Park Ter. EH21: Edin .4A **24**
Parkvale Pl. EH6: Edin .6G **13**
Park Vw. EH20: Loan .6B **40**
EH21: Edin .7K **23**
EH21: Muss .3G **25**
EH32: Pres .6E **14**
Park Vw. E. EH32: Port S .3H **15**
Park Vw. W. EH32: Port S .3H **15**
Parliament Sq. EH1: Edin .4E **4**
Parliament St. EH6: Leith .5E **12**
[illegible]
Parrotshot EH15: Edin .6H **23**
Parsonage EH21: Muss .2F **25**
PARSONS GREEN .3C 22
Parsons Grn. Ter. EH8: Edin .2C **22**
Parsonspool EH19: Bonn .1J **47**
Path Brae EH29: Kltn .2A **16**
Patie's Rd. EH14: Edin .4A **32**
Patriothall EH3: Edin .1F **21** (1A **4**)
Patriothall Gallery .1F 21 (1A 4)
Pattison St. EH6: Leith .5F **13**
Peacock Av. EH19: Bonn .6A **42**
Peacock Ct. EH6: Newh .4C **12**
Peacock Parkway
EH19: Bonn .7A **42**
Peacock Pl. EH19: Bonn .7K **41**
Peacock Ride EH30: S Q'fry .1D **8**
Peacocktail Cl. EH15: Edin .7H **23**
Pearce Av. EH12: Edin .4E **18**
Pearce Gro. EH12: Edin .4E **18**
Pearce Rd. EH12: Edin .4E **18**
Peatville Gdns. EH14: Edin .3J **31**
Peatville Ter. EH14: Edin .3J **31**
Peebles Rd. EH26: Pen .4D **50**
Peel Pentland Cen.
EH20: Loan .4A **40**
Peel Ter. EH9: Edin .7K **21**
Peffer Bank EH16: Edin .7D **22**
Peffer Ind. Est. EH16: Edin .6D **22**
Peffermill Ct. EH16: Edin .7C **22**
Peffermill Ind. Est.
EH16: Edin .7D **22**
Peffermill Rd. EH16: Edin .1B **34**
Peffer Pl. EH16: Edin .7D **22**
Peffer St. EH16: Edin .7D **22**
Peggy's Mill Rd. EH4: Cram .6H **9**
Pembroke Pl. EH12: Edin .4C **20**
Pend, The EH30: S Q'fry .2E **6**
Pendreich Av. EH19: Bonn .5J **41**
Pendreich Dr. EH19: Bonn .5J **41**
Pendreich Gro. EH19: Bonn .4J **41**
Pendreich Ter. EH19: Bonn .5J **41**
Pendreich Vw. EH19: Bonn .5J **41**
Penicuik Rd. EH25: Rosl .3J **45**
PENICUIK .2C 50
Pennywell Cotts. EH4: Edin .4E **10**
Pennywell Ct. EH4: Edin .5E **10**
Pennywell Gdns. EH4: Edin .5D **10**
Pennywell Gro. EH4: Edin .5E **10**
Pennywell Medway
EH4: Edin .5E **10**
Pennywell M. EH4: Edin .5D **10**
Pennywell Pl. EH4: Edin .5E **10**
Pennywell Rd. EH4: Edin .5E **10**
Pennywell Vs. EH4: Edin .4E **10**
Pentland Av. EH13: Edin .6J **31**
EH14: Cur .1H **37**
EH23: Gore .3D **48**
EH26: Pen .1C **50**
Pentland Ct. EH25: Bil .7J **39**
Pentland Cres. EH10: Edin .5E **32**
EH24: Rose .3D **46**
Pentland Dr. EH10: Edin .6D **32**
Pentlandfield Bus. Pk.
EH25: Rosl .7G **39**
Pentland Gdns. EH10: Edin .5E **32**
Pentland Gro. EH10: Edin .5E **32**
Pentland Ind. Est.
EH20: Loan .6K **39**
Pentland Pk. EH20: Loan .5J **39**
Pentland Pl. EH14: Cur .1H **37**
Pentland Rd. EH10: Edin .3G **39**
EH13: Edin .5J **31**
EH19: Bonn .7F **41**
EH20: Loan .4J **39**
Pentlands Science Pk.
EH26: Pen .3G **45**
Pentland Ter. EH10: Edin .4E **32**
(not continuous)
EH26: Pen .1C **50**
Pentland Vw. EH10: Edin .6E **32**
EH14: Cur .1H **37**
EH22: Dalk .3E **42**
Pentland Vw. Ct. EH14: Cur .1J **37**
Pentland Vw. Cres.
EH25: Rosl .3K **45**
Pentland Vw. Pl. EH25: Rosl .3K **45**
Pentland Vw. Rd. EH25: Rosl .3K **45**
EH29: Kltn .2A **16**
Pentland Vw. Ter. EH25: Rosl .3K **45**
Pentland Vs. EH14: J Grn .7E **30**
People's Story Mus., The
.3J 21 (3H 5)
Perdrixknowe EH14: Edin .1B **32**
Perth St. EH3: Edin .1F **21**
Pettigrew's Cl. EH22: Dalk .2C **42**
Peveril Ter. EH16: Edin .4A **34**
Philip Pl. EH26: Pen .7C **44**
Picardy Pl. EH1: Edin .2H **21** (1F **5**)
PICARDY PLACE RDBT. .1G 5
Pier Pl. EH6: Newh .3B **12**
Piersfield Gro. EH8: Edin .2D **22**
Piersfield Pl. EH8: Edin .2D **22**
Piersfield Ter. EH8: Edin .2D **22**
Piershill La. EH8: Edin .2C **22**
Piershill Pl. *EH8: Edin .2C 22*
(off Portobello Rd.)
Piershill Sq. E. EH8: Edin .2D **22**
Piershill Sq. W. EH8: Edin .2C **22**
Piershill Ter. EH8: Edin .2D **22**
PILRIG .6D 12
Pilrig Cotts. EH6: Edin .7E **12**

A-Z Edinburgh 73

Pilrig Gdns. EH6: Edin 7D 12
Pilrig Glebe EH6: Edin 7E 12
Pilrig Hgts. EH6: Edin 7D 12
Pilrig Ho. Cl. EH6: Edin 6D 12
Pilrig Ind. Est. EH6: Edin 6D 12
Pilrig Pl. EH6: Edin 7E 12
Pilrig St. EH6: Edin 6D 12
PILTON 5F 11
Pilton Av. EH5: Edin 5G 11
Pilton Cres. EH5: Edin 5J 11
Pilton Dr. EH5: Edin 5H 11
Pilton Dr. Nth. EH5: Edin 4H 11
Pilton Gdns. EH5: Edin 5H 11
Pilton Loan EH5: Edin 5H 11
Pilton Pk. EH5: Edin 5H 11
Pilton Pl. EH5: Edin 5H 11
Pinegrove Gdns. EH4: Edin 1D 18
Pinewood Pl. EH22: May 7G 43
Pinewood Rd. EH22: May 7G 43
Pinewood Vw. EH22: May 7G 43
Pinkhill EH12: Edin 5H 19
Pinkie Av. EH21: Muss 3G 25
PINKIE BRAES 2H 25
Pinkie Dr. EH21: Muss 3G 25
Pinkie Hill Cres.
    EH21: Muss 3G 25
Pinkie Pl. EH21: Muss 3G 25
Pinkie Rd. EH21: Muss 3F 25
Pinkie Ter. EH21: Muss 3G 25
Pinkie Wlk. EH33: Tran 3G 27
Pipe La. EH15: Port 2G 23
Pipe St. EH15: Port 2G 23
Pirniefield Bank EH6: Edin 6H 13
Pirniefield Gdns. EH6: Edin 6H 13
Pirniefield Gro. EH6: Edin 6H 13
Pirniefield Pl. EH6: Edin 6H 13
Pirniefield Ter. EH6: Edin 6H 13
Pirrie St. EH6: Edin 6E 12
Pitlochry Pl. EH7: Edin 1A 22
Pitsligo Rd. EH10: Edin 7F 21
Pittencrieff Ct. EH21: Muss 2H 25
Pitt St. EH6: Edin 5C 12
Pittville St. EH15: Port 3H 23
Pittville St. La. EH15: Port 3H 23
Place Charente EH22: Dalk 2E 42
Playfair Steps EH1: Edin 4D 4
Playhouse Theatre 2J 21 (1G 5)
Pleasance EH8: Edin 4J 21 (4G 5)
Plewlandcroft EH30: S Q'fry 1G 7
Plewlands Av. EH10: Edin 2D 32
Plewlands Gdns. EH10: Edin 2D 32
Plewlands Pl. EH30: S Q'fry 1G 7
Plewlands Ter. EH10: Edin 2D 32
Pleydell Pl. EH16: Edin 4B 34
Plough La. EH33: Tran 2H 27
Plummer Ct. EH22: Dalk 1C 42
Poet's Glen EH14: Cur 1K 37
Police Info. Cen. & Exhibition
    . . . . .3H 21 (4F 5)
    (off High St.)
Pollard Glebe EH11: Edin 7J 19
Pollock Halls of Residence
    EH16: Edin 6A 22
Polson Gdns. EH33: Tran 2F 27
POLTONHALL 6G 41
POLTON 7E 40
Polton Av. Rd. EH19: Bonn 7F 41
Polton Bank EH18: Las 7D 40
Polton Bank Ter. EH18: Las 7E 40
Polton Cotts. EH18: Las 7D 40
Polton Ct. EH19: Bonn 6H 41
Polton Dr. EH18: Las 7F 41
Polton Gdns. EH18: Las 6G 41
Polton Pl. EH19: Bonn 6H 41
Polton Rd. EH18: Las 6G 41
    (Eskdale Dr.)
    EH18: Las 7D 40
    (Polton Bank)
    EH20: Loan 6C 40
Polton Rd. W. EH18: Las 7E 40
Polton St. EH19: Bonn 7H 41
Polton Ter. EH18: Las 6G 41
Polton Va. EH20: Loan 7C 40
Polwarth Cres. EH11: Edin 6E 20
    EH32: Pres 6E 14
Polwarth Gdns. EH11: Edin 6D 20
Polwarth Gro. EH11: Edin 6D 20
Polwarth Pk. EH11: Edin 6D 20
Polwarth Pl. EH11: Edin 6D 20
Polwarth Ter. EH11: Edin 1C 32
    EH32: Pres 6E 14
Pomathorn Bank EH26: Pen 3D 50

Pomathorn Rd. EH26: Pen 3D 50
Ponton St. EH3: Edin 5F 21 (7B 4)
Poplar La. EH6: Leith 5F 13
Poplar Pk. EH32: Port S 4H 15
Poplar Path EH20: Loan 6J 39
    (off Nivensknowe Pk.)
Poplar St. EH22: May 7G 43
Poplar Ter. EH19: Bonn 7H 41
Port Edgar Marina
    (Water Sports Cen.) 1F 7
Porterfield Rd. EH4: Edin 7H 11
Portgower Pl. EH4: Edin 1E 20
Port Hamilton
    EH3: Edin 4F 21 (6A 4)
Portland Pl. EH6: Leith 4D 12
    (off Lindsay Rd.)
Portland St. EH6: Newh 4D 12
Portland Ter. EH6: Newh 4D 12
PORTOBELLO 3H 23
Portobello High St.
    EH15: Port 2G 23
Portobello Indoor Bowls &
    Leisure Club 2G 23
Portobello Rd. EH8: Edin 2C 22
Portobello Swimming Cen. 3J 23
Portsburgh Sq. EH1: Edin 5C 4
PORT SETON 3H 15
Post Rd. EH33: Tran 1F 27
Potterrow EH8: Edin 4H 21 (6F 5)
Potterrow Port EH1: Edin 5F 5
Potter's Path EH33: Tran 2G 27
Pottery, The EH15: Port 2G 23
Povert Rd. EH19: Bonn 4B 48
    EH23: Gore 4B 48
Powderhall Brae EH7: Edin 6C 12
Powderhall Rigg EH7: Edin 6C 12
Powderhall Rd. EH7: Edin 7B 12
Powdermill Brae EH23: Gore 7F 49
Powerleague Soccer Cen.
    Portobello 2G 23
    Sighthill 1F 31
PRESTON 6E 14
Preston Av. EH32: Pres 6F 15
Preston Ct. EH32: Pres 7D 14
Preston Cres. EH32: Pres 5F 15
Preston Cross Cotts.
    EH32: Pres 6E 14
PRESTONFIELD 7A 22
Prestonfield Av. EH16: Edin 7A 22
Prestonfield Bank EH16: Edin 7A 22
Prestonfield Cres.
    EH16: Edin 1A 34
Prestonfield Gdns.
    EH16: Edin 7A 22
Prestonfield Rd. EH16: Edin 7A 22
Prestongrange Industrial
    Heritage Mus. 7A 14
Prestongrange Rd.
    EH32: Pres 6B 14
Prestongrange Ter.
    EH32: Pres 7C 14
Prestonhall Cres.
    EH24: Rose 4D 46
Prestonhall Rd. EH24: Rose 4D 46
Preston Links Shop. Cen.
    EH32: Pres 5D 14
PRESTONPANS 6C 14
Prestonpans Station (Rail) 7E 14
Preston Rd. EH32: Pres 7D 14
Preston St. EH24: Rose 4D 46
Preston Ter. EH32: Pres 6F 15
Preston Twr. EH32: Pres 6D 14
Priestfield Av. EH16: Edin 7B 22
Priestfield Cres. EH16: Edin 7B 22
Priestfield Gdns. EH16: Edin 7B 22
Priestfield Gro. EH16: Edin 6A 22
Priestfield Rd. EH16: Edin 7A 22
Priestfield Rd. Nth.
    EH16: Edin 6A 22
Priesthill Pl. EH16: Edin 6B 34
Priesthill St. EH16: Edin 6B 34
Primrose Bank Rd.
    EH5: Edin 4A 12
Primrose Cres. EH22: Dalk 3E 42
Primrose Dr. EH30: S Q'fry 7E 8
Primrose Gdns. EH30: S Q'fry 2H 7
Primrose Pl. EH6: Edin 6F 13
Primrose Ter. EH11: Edin 6C 20
    EH22: Dalk 3E 42
Prince Regent St.
    EH6: Newh 4D 12

Princes Ct. EH3: Edin 6B 4
Princes Mall
    EH1: Edin 3H 21 (3E 4)
PRINCESS ALEXANDRIA
    EYE PAVILION 4G 21 (6D 4)
Princes St. EH2: Edin 3F 21 (4A 4)
Printmakers Workshop & Gallery
    . . . . .1J 21 (1G 5)
    (off Gayfield Cl.)
Priory Gro. EH30: S Q'fry 2G 7
Private Rd. EH23: Gore 7E 48
Promenade EH15: Port 7K 13
    EH21: Muss 1D 24
Promenade, The
    EH32: Port S 3H 15
Promenade Ter. EH15: Port 2G 23
Prospect Bank Cres.
    EH6: Edin 6G 13
Prospect Bank Gdns.
    EH6: Edin 7G 13
Prospect Bank Gro.
    EH6: Edin 6H 13
Prospect Bank Pl. EH6: Edin 6H 13
Prospect Bank Rd. EH6: Edin 6G 13
Prospect Bank Ter. EH6: Edin 6H 13
Provost Haugh EH14: Cur 7E 30
Provost Milne Gro.
    EH30: S Q'fry 3H 7
Pryde Av. EH19: Bonn 6G 41
Pryde Ter. EH19: Bonn 6G 41
Pypers Wynd EH32: Pres 5D 14

Real Mary King's Close, The
.... .3H 21 (4E 4)
(off High St.)
Redbraes Gro. EH7: Edin 6C 12
Redbraes Pl. EH7: Edin 6C 12
Redburn Rd. EH32: Pres 6C 14
Redburn Rd. Nth.
   EH32: Pres 6C 14
Redcroft St. EH22: Dan 4G 35
Redford Av. EH13: Edin 6K 31
Redford Bank EH13: Edin 6A 32
Redford Cres. EH13: Edin 6A 32
Redford Dr. EH13: Edin 6K 31
Redford Gdns. EH13: Edin 6B 32
Redford Gro. EH13: Edin 6B 32
Redford Loan EH13: Edin 6K 31
Redford Neuk EH13: Edin 6B 32
Redford Pl. EH13: Edin 5B 32
Redford Rd. EH13: Edin 5K 31
Redford Ter. EH13: Edin 6A 32
Redford Wlk. EH13: Edin 6K 31
Red Fox Cres. EH26: Pen 5E 44
Redgauntlet Ter. EH16: Edin ..3C 34
REDHALL 3K 31
Redhall Av. EH14: Edin 2J 31
Redhall Bank Rd.
   EH14: Edin 3K 31
Redhall Cres. EH14: Edin 2J 31
Redhall Dr. EH14: Edin 2J 31
Redhall Gdns. EH14: Edin 2J 31
Redhall Gro. EH14: Edin 2J 31
Redhall Ho. Dr. EH14: Edin ..3K 31
Redhall Pl. EH14: Edin 2J 31
Redhall Rd. EH14: Edin 2J 31
Redhall Vw. EH14: Edin 2J 31
Redheugh Loan EH23: Gore ...4E 48
Redheughs Av. EH12: Edin ...7C 18
Redheughs Rigg EH12: Edin ..6C 18
Redwood Gro. EH22: Newt 1C 48
Redwood Wlk. EH22: Newt 1C 48
Reed Dr. EH22: Newt 7D 42
Reekies Ct. EH8: Edin ..4J 21 (6G 5)
Regent Pl. EH7: Edin 2A 22
Regent Rd. EH7: Edin ..2J 21 (2G 5)
Regent St. EH15: Port 3H 23
Regent St. La. EH15: Port 3H 23
Regent Ter. EH7: Edin ..2J 21 (2H 5)
Regent Ter. M.
   EH7: Edin 2K 21 (2J 5)
Regis Ct. EH4: Cram 6J 9
Register Pl. EH2: Edin ...2H 21 (2E 4)
Reid Concert Hall & Mus.
   ....4H 21 (6E 5)
Reid's Cl. EH8: Edin ..3K 21 (3J 5)
Reid's Ct. EH8: Edin ..3K 21 (3J 5)
Reid Ter. EH3: Edin 1E 20
Relugas Gdns. EH9: Edin 1J 33
Relugas Pl. EH9: Edin 1J 33
Relugas Rd. EH9: Edin 1J 33
Rennies Ri. EH6: Leith 4F 13
Research Av. Nth.
   EH14: Cur 4A 30
Research Av. Sth.
   EH14: Cur 4B 30
RESTALRIG 1C 22
Restalrig Av. EH7: Edin 2C 22
Restalrig Cir. EH7: Edin 7H 13
Restalrig Cres. EH7: Edin 7H 13
Restalrig Dr. EH7: Edin 1C 22
Restalrig Gdns. EH7: Edin 1C 22
Restalrig Ho. EH7: Edin 1C 22
Restalrig Pk. EH7: Edin 7G 13
Restalrig Rd. EH6: Edin 6G 13
Restalrig Rd. Sth.
   EH7: Edin 7H 13
Restalrig Sq. EH7: Edin 7H 13
Restalrig Ter. EH6: Edin 6F 13
RICCARTON 5B 30
Riccarton Av. EH14: Cur 7B 30
Riccarton Cres. EH14: Cur 7C 30
Riccarton Dr. EH14: Cur 7C 30
Riccarton Gro. EH14: Cur 7C 30
Riccarton Mains Rd.
   EH14: Cur 3B 30
Richard Corsie Leisure Cen. ...5K 23
Richmond La.
   EH8: Edin 4J 21 (6G 5)
Richmond Pl.
   EH8: Edin 4J 21 (6G 5)
Richmond Ter. EH11: Edin 4E 20
Riddle's Ct. EH1: Edin 4E 4
Riding Pk. EH4: Cram 6J 9

Riego St. EH3: Edin 4F 21 (6B 4)
Riggonhead Ct. EH33: Tran 1H 27
Riggonhead Gdns.
   EH33: Tran 1H 27
Rigley Ter. EH32: Pres 7C 14
Rillbank Cres. EH9: Edin 6H 21
Rillbank Ter. EH9: Edin 6H 21
Ringans Way EH32: Pres 6C 14
   (off Inch Vw.)
Ringwood Pl. EH16: Edin 4B 34
Rintoul Pl. EH3: Edin 1F 21
Riselaw Cres. EH10: Edin 5E 32
Riselaw Pl. EH10: Edin 4E 32
Riselaw Rd. EH10: Edin 4E 32
Riselaw Ter. EH10: Edin 4E 32
Ritchie Pl. EH11: Edin 6D 20
River Almond Wlk. EH4: Cram ..6G 9
River Gore Gro. EH23: Gore ...6E 48
River Gore Rd. EH23: Gore 6E 48
River Gore Vw. EH23: Gore ...6E 48
Riversdale Cres. EH12: Edin ...5A 20
Riversdale Gro. EH12: Edin 4A 20
Riversdale Rd. EH12: Edin 4A 20
Riverside EH4: Cram 4J 9
   EH28: Nbdge 5A 16
Riverside Gdns. EH21: Muss ..3D 24
Riverside Rd. EH30: S Q'fry ...6E 8
Roanshead Rd. EH22: East 5E 42
Robb's Loan EH14: Edin 7A 20
Robb's Loan Gro. EH14: Edin ..7A 20
Robert Burns Dr. EH16: Edin ..3A 34
Robert Burns M. EH22: Dalk ...2F 43
Robert De Quincy Pl.
   EH32: Pres 7D 14
   (off Northfield Ct.)
Robert Smillie Av.
   EH22: May 1G 49
Robertson Av. EH11: Edin 6B 20
Robertson Bank EH23: Gore ...7F 49
Robertson Dr. EH33: Tran 1H 27
Robertson's Cl.
   EH1: Edin 4J 21 (5G 5)
   EH22: Dalk 2C 42
Robertson's Ct.
   EH8: Edin 3K 21 (3J 5)
Rocheid Pk. EH4: Edin 6J 11
Rocheid Path EH3: Edin 7A 12
Rochester Ter. EH10: Edin 7E 20
Rockville Ter. EH19: Bonn 5H 41
Roddinglaw Bus. Pk.
   EH12: Edin 1H 29
Roddinglaw Rd. EH12: Edin ...7H 17
Rodney Pl. EH3: Edin 1G 21
Rodney St. EH7: Edin 1G 21
Romero Pl. EH16: Edin 6K 21
Rope Wlk. EH32: Pres 6C 14
Rosabelle Rd. EH5: Rosl 3K 45
Rose Av. EH19: Bonn 7K 41
Rosebank Cotts.
   EH3: Edin 4E 20 (6A 4)
Rosebank Gdns. EH5: Edin 5K 11
Rosebank Gro. EH5: Edin 5K 11
Rosebank Rd. EH5: Edin 5K 11
Rosebery Av. EH30: S Q'fry ...2H 7
Rosebery Ct. EH30: S Q'fry ...2H 7
Rosebery Cres. EH12: Edin ...4D 20
   EH23: Gore 7E 48
Rosebery Cres. La.
   EH12: Edin 4D 20
ROSEBURN 4B 20
Roseburn Av. EH12: Edin 4B 20
Roseburn Cliff EH12: Edin 4C 20
Roseburn Cres. EH12: Edin 4B 20
Roseburn Dr. EH12: Edin 4B 20
Roseburn Gdns. EH12: Edin ...4B 20
Roseburn Maltings
   EH12: Edin 4C 20
Roseburn Pl. EH12: Edin 4B 20
Roseburn St. EH12: Edin 5B 20
Roseburn Ter. EH12: Edin 4B 20
Rose Cotts. EH19: Bonn 7K 41
Rose Ct. EH4: Edin 6B 10
Rosedale Ct. EH24: Rose 6D 46
Rosedale Gro. EH24: Rose 6D 46
Rosedale Neuk EH24: Rose 5D 46
Rosefield Av. EH15: Port 3G 23
Rosefield Av. La. EH15: Port ...3G 23
Rosefield Pl. La. EH15: Port ...3G 23
Rosefield St. EH15: Port 3G 23

Rose Gdns. EH19: Bonn 7K 41
Rose Gro. EH19: Bonn 7K 41
Rose La. EH30: S Q'fry 1G 7
Rosemount Bldgs.
   EH3: Edin 4E 20 (6A 4)
Rosemount M. EH32: Pres 5D 14
   (off Mill Wynd)
Roseneath Pl. EH9: Edin 6H 21
Roseneath Ter. EH9: Edin 6H 21
Rose Neuk EH19: Bonn 7K 41
Rose Pk. EH5: Edin 5A 12
   EH19: Bonn 7K 41
Rose Path EH19: Bonn 7K 41
Rose Pl. EH19: Bonn 7K 41
Rose St. EH2: Edin 3F 21 (3B 4)
Rose St. Nth. La.
   EH2: Edin 3F 21 (3B 4)
   (not continuous)
Rose St. Sth. La.
   EH2: Edin 3F 21 (3B 4)
   (not continuous)
Rose Ter. EH19: Bonn 7K 41
Rosevale Pl. EH6: Edin 6G 13
Rosevale Ter. EH6: Edin 6F 13
Roseville Gdns. EH5: Edin 4B 12
Rose Way EH19: Bonn 7K 41
ROSEWELL 4D 46
Rosewell By-Pass
   EH24: Rose 4D 46
Rosewell Rd. EH19: Bonn 2F 47
ROSLIN 3K 45
Roslin Glen Country Pk. 4A 46
Ross Cres. EH33: Tran 3H 27
Ross Gdns. EH9: Edin 1J 33
Rossglen Ct. EH25: Rosl 3A 46
Rosshill Ter. EH30: Dalm 2J 7
Rossie Pl. EH7: Edin ...1K 21 (1K 5)
Rosslyn Chapel 3B 46
Rosslyn Cres. EH6: Edin 7D 12
ROSSLYNLEE HOSPITAL 7K 45
Rosslyn Ter. EH6: Edin 7D 12
Ross Open Air Theatre
   ....3G 21 (3C 4)
Ross Pl. EH9: Edin 1K 33
   EH22: Newt 7D 42
Ross Rd. EH16: Edin 2K 33
Rothesay M. EH3: Edin 3D 20
Rothesay Pl. EH12: Edin 3E 20
   EH21: Muss 3F 25
Rothesay Ter. EH3: Edin 3E 20
Roull Gro. EH12: Edin 6F 19
Roull Pl. EH12: Edin 6G 19
Roull Rd. EH12: Edin 6F 19
Rowallan Cl. EH12: Edin 6C 18
   (off Craigievar Wynd)
Rowan Gdns. EH19: Bonn 7H 41
Rowanhill Cl. EH32: Port S 4H 15
Rowanhill Dr. EH32: Port S 4H 15
Rowanhill Gro. EH32: Port S ...4H 15
Rowanhill Pk. EH32: Port S 4G 15
Rowanhill Way EH32: Port S ...4H 15
Rowan Tree Av. EH14: Cur 1G 37
Rowan Tree Gro. EH14: Cur ...2G 37
Rowantree Rd. EH22: May 6G 43
Roxburgh Pl.
   EH8: Edin 4J 21 (5G 5)
Roxburgh's Cl. EH1: Edin 4E 4
Roxburgh St.
   EH8: Edin 4J 21 (5G 5)
Roxy Art House, The 5G 5
Royal Botanic Garden & Arboretum
   ....7A 12
Royal British Legion Scotland
   (Branch Office & Club) 4G 5
Royal Cir. EH3: Edin ...2F 21 (1B 4)
Royal Commonwealth Pool 6K 21
Royal Ct. EH26: Pen 7B 44
Royal Cres. EH3: Edin 1G 21
ROYAL EDINBURGH HOSPITAL
   ....1E 32
Royal Elizabeth Yd. EH30: Kltn ..4H 7
Royal Forth Yacht Club 3J 11
Royal Highland Showground
   ....5E 16
ROYAL HOSPITAL FOR
   SICK CHILDREN, THE 6H 21
ROYAL INFIRMARY OF EDINBURGH
   ....3E 34
Royal Lyceum Theatre 5B 4
Royal Mile 4F 5
Royal Mus. 4H 21 (5F 5)
Royal Observatory & Vis. Cen.
   ....2H 33

Royal Pk. Pl. EH8: Edin 2B 22
Royal Pk. Ter. EH8: Edin 2B 22
Royal Scots Greys Memorial ...3C 4
Royal Scots Monument 3D 4
Royal Scottish Academy
   ....3G 21 (3D 4)
Royal Society of Edinburgh 3C 4
Royal Ter. EH7: Edin ...2J 21 (1G 5)
Royal Ter. M.
   EH7: Edin 2K 21 (1J 5)
ROYAL VICTORIA HOSPITAL ..1C 20
Royston Mains Av. EH5: Edin ..4G 11
Royston Mains Cl. EH5: Edin ..4H 11
Royston Mains Cres.
   EH5: Edin 4G 11
Royston Mains Gdns.
   EH5: Edin 4H 11
Royston Mains Grn.
   EH5: Edin 4H 11
Royston Mains Pl. EH5: Edin ..4G 11
Royston Mains Rd.
   EH5: Edin 4H 11
Royston Mains St. EH5: Edin ..4G 11
Rullion Grn. Av. EH26: Pen ...7B 44
Rullion Grn. Cres. EH26: Pen ..7B 44
Rullion Grn. Gro. EH26: Pen ...7B 44
Rullion Grn. Ter. EH26: Pen ...2A 50
Ruskin Pl. EH22: May 1G 49
Russell Gdns. EH12: Edin 4C 20
Russell Pl. EH5: Edin 4A 12
Russell Rd. EH11: Edin 5C 20
   EH12: Edin 4C 20
Rustic Cotts. EH13: Edin 5K 31
Rutherford Dr. EH16: Edin 3B 34
Ruthven Pl. EH16: Edin 3B 34
Rutland Ct. EH1: Edin 4F 21 (5A 4)
Rutland Ct. La.
   EH3: Edin 4F 21 (5A 4)
Rutland Pl. EH1: Edin 4A 4
Rutland Sq. EH1: Edin ...3F 21 (4A 4)
Rutland St. EH1: Edin ...3F 21 (4A 4)
Ryehill Av. EH6: Edin 7G 13
Ryehill Gdns. EH6: Edin 6G 13
Ryehill Gro. EH6: Edin 7G 13
Ryehill Pl. EH6: Edin 6G 13
Ryehill Ter. EH6: Edin 6G 13

S

Saddletree Loan EH16: Edin ...2C 34
St Albans Rd. EH9: Edin 1H 33
St Andrew Pl. EH6: Leith 6F 13
St Andrew Sq.
   EH2: Edin 2H 21 (2E 4)
St Andrew St. EH22: Dalk 2C 42
St Annes EH22: Newt 1C 48
St Ann's Av. EH18: Las 7E 40
St Ann's Path EH18: Las 7E 40
St Anthony La. EH6: Leith 5E 12
St Anthony Pl. EH6: Edin 5E 12
St Anthony St. EH6: Leith 5E 12
St Bernard's Cres.
   EH4: Edin 2E 20 (1A 4)
St Bernard's Row EH4: Edin ..1F 21
St Catherine's Gdns.
   EH12: Edin 5J 19
St Catherine's Mnr.
   EH12: Edin 5H 19
   (off St Catherine's Gdns.)
St Catherine's Pl. EH9: Edin ..6J 21
St Cecilia's Hall 4G 5
St Clair Av. EH6: Edin 7F 13
St Clair Cres. EH25: Rosl 3A 46
St Clair Pl. EH6: Edin 7F 13
St Clair Rd. EH6: Edin 7F 13
St Clair St. EH6: Edin 7F 13
St Clair Ter. EH10: Edin 2D 32
St Clement's Cres.
   EH21: Wall 4K 25
St Clement's Gdns. Nth.
   EH21: Wall 4K 25
St Clement's Gdns. Sth.
   EH21: Wall 4K 25
St Clement's Ter. EH21: Wall ..4K 25
St Colme St. EH3: Edin ..2F 21 (3A 4)
ST COLUMBA'S HOSPICE 4K 11
St Cuthbert's Church 4B 4
St David's EH22: Newt 1C 48
St David's Pl. EH3: Edin 4E 20
St David's Ter. EH3: Edin 4E 20

Strathearn Pl.—Wardieburn St. E.

Strathearn Pl. EH9: Edin 7F 21
Strathearn Rd. EH9: Edin 7G 21
Strathesk Gro. EH26: Pen 1E 50
Strathesk Pl. EH26: Pen 1E 50
Strathesk Rd. EH26: Pen 1E 50
Strathfillan Rd. EH9: Edin 7G 21
Strawberry Bank EH22: Dalk 4A 42
Stuart Ct. EH12: Edin 3D 18
Stuart Cres. EH12: Edin 3D 18
Stuart Grn. EH12: Edin 3D 18
Stuart Pk. EH12: Edin 3D 18
Stuart Sq. EH12: Edin 3D 18
Stuart Wynd EH12: Edin 3D 18
Succoth Av. EH12: Edin 3B 20
Succoth Ct. EH12: Edin 3B 20
Succoth Gdns. EH12: Edin 3B 20
Succoth Hgts. EH12: Edin 3B 20
Succoth Pk. EH12: Edin 3A 20
Succoth Pl. EH12: Edin 3B 20
Suffolk Rd. EH16: Edin 1K 33
Suffolk Rd. La. EH16: Edin 1K 33
Sugarhouse Cl. EH8: Edin 4H 5
Summer Bank EH3: Edin 1G 21
Summerfield Gdns. EH6: Edin 6G 13
Summerfield Pl. EH6: Edin 6G 13
Summerhall EH9: Edin 5J 21
Summerhall Pl. *EH9: Edin 6J 21*
(off Summerhall)
Summerhall Sq. EH9: Edin 6J 21
Summerlee EH32: Pres 6C 14
Summer Pl. EH3: Edin 7A 12
Summerside Pl. EH6: Newh 5C 12
Summerside St. EH6: Newh 5C 12
Summertrees Ct. EH16: Edin 3B 34
SUNBURY 3D 20
Sunbury M. EH4: Edin 3D 20
Sunbury Pl. EH4: Edin 3D 20
Sunbury St. EH4: Edin 3D 20
Sunnybank EH7: Edin 2B 22
Sunnybank Pl. EH7: Edin 2B 22
Sunnybank Ter. *EH7: Edin 2A 22*
(off Lwr. London Rd.)
Sunnyside EH7: Edin 1A 22
Suntrap 2A 30
Surgeon's Hall EH8: Edin 5G 5
Sutherland St. EH12: Edin 4C 20
Suttieslea Cres. EH22: Newt 7E 42
Suttieslea Dr. EH22: Newt 7E 42
Suttieslea Pl. EH22: Newt 7E 42
Suttieslea Rd. EH22: Newt 7E 42
Suttieslea Wlk. EH22: Newt 7E 42
Swan Cres. EH23: Gore 5E 48
Swanfield EH6: Edin 5E 12
Swan Rd. EH33: Tran 3G 27
Swan Spring Av. EH10: Edin 5D 32
SWANSTON 7E 32
Swanston Av. EH10: Edin 7E 32
Swanston Cres. EH10: Edin 7E 32
Swanston Dr. EH10: Edin 1F 39
Swanston Gdns. EH10: Edin 7E 32
Swanston Grn. EH10: Edin 7E 32
Swanston Gro. EH10: Edin 1F 39
Swanston Loan EH10: Edin 7E 32
Swanston Muir EH13: Edin 7C 32
Swanston Pk. EH10: Edin 7E 32
Swanston Pl. EH10: Edin 7E 32
Swanston Rd. EH10: Edin 7D 32
Swanston Row EH10: Edin 7E 32
Swanston Ter. EH10: Edin 7F 33
Swanston Vw. EH10: Edin 7E 32
Swanston Way EH10: Edin 7E 32
Sycamore Av. EH32: Port S 4H 15
Sycamore Gdns. EH12: Edin 5F 19
Sycamore Path *EH20: Loan 6J 39*
(off Nivensknowe Pk.)
Sycamore Rd. EH22: May 7G 43
Sycamore Ter. EH12: Edin 5G 19
Sydney Pk. EH7: Edin 1E 22
Sydney Pl. EH7: Edin 1E 22
Sydney Ter. EH7: Edin 1E 22
Sylvan Pl. EH9: Edin 6H 21
Syme Cres. EH10: Edin 4C 32
Syme Pl. EH10: Edin 4C 32
Syme Rigg EH10: Edin 4C 32

T

Tait Dr. EH26: Pen 2D 50
Tait St. EH22: Dalk 2C 42
Talbot Rice Gallery 4H 21 (5F 5)
Talisman Pl. EH16: Edin 3B 34
Tanfield EH3: Edin 7B 12
Tantallon Pl. EH9: Edin 6H 21
Tartan Weaving Mill & Exhibition 4D 4
Tarvit St. EH3: Edin 5F 21 (7B 4)
Taylor Gdns. EH6: Leith 5E 12
Taylor Pl. EH7: Edin 2A 22
EH22: Dalk 3E 42
Tay St. EH11: Edin 6D 20
Telfer Subway EH11: Edin 5D 20
Telferton EH7: Edin 2F 23
Telford Dr. EH4: Edin 7G 11
Telford Gdns. EH4: Edin 7G 11
Telford Pl. EH4: Edin 7G 11
Telford Rd. EH4: Edin 1K 19
Templar's Cramond
EH4: Cram 6H 9
Templeland Gro. EH12: Edin 4F 19
Templeland Rd. EH12: Edin 4E 18
Temple Pk. Cres.
EH11: Edin 6D 20
Tennant St. EH6: Edin 6E 12
Tenth St. EH22: Newt 7D 42
Terrars Cft. EH8: Edin 5K 21 (7J 5)
Terregles EH26: Pen 1B 50
Teviotbank Ho. EH16: Edin 1G 35
Teviotdale Pl. EH3: Edin 7A 12
Teviot Gro. EH26: Pen 7D 44
Teviot Pl. EH1: Edin 4H 21 (6E 4)
Third Gait EH14: Cur 5A 30
Third St. EH22: Newt 2C 48
(not continuous)
Thirlestane La. EH9: Edin 7G 21
Thirlestane Rd. EH9: Edin 6G 21
Thistle Ct. EH2: Edin 2D 4
Thistle Pl. EH11: Edin 6E 20
Thistle St. EH2: Edin 2G 21 (2C 4)
Thistle St. Nth. E. La.
EH2: Edin 2G 21 (2D 4)
Thistle St. Nth. W. La.
EH2: Edin 2G 21 (2C 4)
Thistle St. Sth. E. La.
EH2: Edin 2G 21 (2D 4)
Thistle St. Sth. W. La.
EH2: Edin 2G 21 (2C 4)
Thomson Cres. EH14: Cur 7D 30
EH32: Port S 3G 15
Thomson Dr. EH14: Cur 7D 30
Thomson Gro. EH14: Cur 7D 30
Thomson Rd. EH14: Cur 7D 30
Thomson's Ct. EH1: Edin 5D 4
Thorburn Gro. EH13: Edin 6A 32
Thorburn Rd. EH13: Edin 6K 31
Thornburn Ter. EH26: Pen 3C 50
Thornhall Cotts. EH22: Dalk 1D 42
Thornton Rd. EH24: Rose 5D 46
Thorntree Cres. EH32: Pres 6F 15
Thorntreeside EH6: Edin 7F 13
Thorntree St. EH6: Edin 6E 12
Thornville Ter. EH6: Edin 7F 13
Thornybank EH22: Dalk 1E 42
Thornybank Ind. Est.
EH22: Dalk 1F 43
Thorny Bauk EH3: Edin 4F 21 (6B 4)
(not continuous)
Thornyhall EH22: Dalk 1E 42
Threipmuir Av. EH14: Bal 5E 36
Threipmuir Gdns. EH14: Bal 5E 36
Threipmuir Pl. EH14: Bal 5E 36
Timber Bush EH6: Leith 4F 13
(not continuous)
Timmins Ct. EH28: Rat 2D 28
Tinto Pl. EH6: Edin 6D 12
Tipperlinn Rd. EH10: Edin 7E 20
Toddshill Rd. EH29: Kltn 2A 16
Tolbooth Wynd EH6: Leith 5E 12
TOLL CROSS 4F 21 (6B 4)
Toll Cross Junc. 7B 4
Torduff Rd. EH13: Edin 7J 31
Torphichen Pl. EH3: Edin 4E 20
Torphichen St. EH3: Edin 4E 20
Torphin Bank EH13: Edin 7H 31
Torphin Rd. EH13: Edin 7H 31
Torrance Pk. EH4: Edin 2E 18
Torsonce Rd. EH22: Dalk 3B 42
Toscana Ct. EH16: Dan 4G 35
Tourist Info. Cen.
Edinburgh 3H 21 (4F 5)
Edinburgh Airport 3F 17
Princes Mall 3H 21 (3F 5)
Toward Ct. *EH12: Edin 4C 18*
(off Craigievar Wynd)
Tower Pl. EH6: Leith 4F 13
Tower St. EH6: Leith 4F 13
Tower Wharf EH6: Leith 4F 13
Tower Wynd EH6: Leith 4F 13
Trafalgar La. EH6: Edin 5C 12
Trafalgar St. EH6: Edin 5D 12
TRANENT 2H 27
Tranent By-Pass EH33: Tran 2D 26
Tranent Rd. EH33: Elph 7F 27
Traprain Ter. EH20: Loan 6C 40
Traquair Pk. E. EH12: Edin 5H 19
Traquair Pk. W. EH12: Edin 5G 19
Traverse Theatre 4F 21 (5B 4)
Trelawney Ter. EH26: Pen 6E 44
Trench Knowe EH10: Edin 7E 32
Tressilian Gdns. EH16: Edin 3A 34
TRINITY 4A 12
Trinity Ct. EH5: Edin 5A 12
Trinity Cres. EH5: Edin 3A 12
Trinity Gro. EH5: Edin 4A 12
Trinity Mains EH5: Edin 5A 12
Trinity Pk. Ho. EH5: Edin 5A 12
Trinity Rd. EH5: Edin 4A 12
Trinity Way EH5: Edin 5A 12
Tron Church *3H 21 (4F 5)*
(off Hunter Sq.)
Tron Sq. EH1: Edin 4F 5
Trotter Haugh EH9: Edin 1H 33
Trunk's Cl. EH1: Edin 4G 5
Tryst Pk. EH10: Edin 7D 32
Tunnel, The EH14: Edin 3J 31
Turlies, The EH13: Edin 5J 31
Turner Av. EH14: Bal 2D 36
Turner Pk. EH14: Bal 2D 36
Turnhouse Farm Rd.
EH12: Edin A 2J 17
Turnhouse Rd.
EH12: Edin, Edin A 2H 17
Turret Gdns. EH32: Pres 7D 14
Tweeddale Ct. EH1: Edin 4G 5
Tweedsmuir Ho. EH16: Edin 1F 35
Tyler's Acre Av. EH12: Edin 6G 19
Tyler's Acre Gdns.
EH12: Edin 6G 19
Tyler's Acre Rd. EH12: Edin 6G 19
Tynecastle La. EH11: Edin 6C 20
Tynecastle Ter. EH11: Edin 6C 20
Tytler Ct. EH8: Edin 2A 22
Tytler Gdns. EH8: Edin 2K 21 (2K 5)

U

UCI Cinema
Fort Kinnaird 7J 23
UGC Cinema
Edinburgh 5E 20
Ulster Cres. EH8: Edin 3C 22
Ulster Dr. EH8: Edin 3D 22
Ulster Gdns. EH8: Edin 4D 22
Ulster Gro. EH8: Edin 4D 22
Ulster Ter. EH8: Edin 4D 22
Union Pk. EH19: Bonn 6H 41
Union Pl. EH1: Edin 1G 5
Union St. EH1: Edin 1H 21 (1F 5)
Upper Bow EH1: Edin 3H 21 (4E 4)
Upper Broomieknowe
EH18: Las 6G 41
Up. Coltbridge Ter.
EH12: Edin 3C 20
Upper Craigour EH16: Edin 3E 34
Up. Craigour Way
EH16: Edin 3D 34
Up. Cramond Ct. EH4: Cram 6J 9
Upper Damside EH4: Edin 3D 20
Up. Dean Ter.
EH4: Edin 2E 20 (1A 4)
Up. Gilmore Pl.
EH3: Edin 5F 21 (7A 4)
Up. Gilmore Ter. EH3: Edin 5F 21
Up. Gray St. EH9: Edin 6J 21
Up. Greenside La.
EH1: Edin 2J 21 (1G 5)
Up. Grove Pl. EH3: Edin 5E 20
Upper Hermitage EH6: Edin 6F 13
Usher Hall 5B 4

V

Valleyfield EH26: Pen 3D 50
Valleyfield Rd. EH26: Pen 3D 50
Valleyfield St.
EH3: Edin 5F 21 (7B 4)
Vanburgh Pl. EH6: Edin 6F 13
Vancluse Pl. EH26: Pen 3C 50
Vandeleur Av. EH7: Edin 1E 22
Vandeleur Gro. EH7: Edin 2E 22
Vandeleur Pl. EH7: Edin 1E 22
Veitch's Sq. EH4: Edin 1F 21
Vennel EH1: Edin 4G 21 (5D 4)
Vennel, The EH30: S Q'fry 1H 7
Ventnor Pl. EH9: Edin 7A 22
Ventnor Ter. EH9: Edin 7K 21
Vernon Cotts. *EH15: Port 3H 23*
(off Bellfield St.)
Vexhim Pk. EH15: Edin 6H 23
Victoria Gdns. EH22: Newt 7B 42
Victoria Quay EH6: Leith 4E 12
Victoria Rd. EH22: Newt 7B 42
Victoria St. EH1: Edin 4H 21 (5E 4)
EH24: Rose 4D 46
Victoria Ter. EH1: Edin 5D 4
EH21: Muss 2G 25
Victor Pk. Ter. EH12: Edin 4F 19
Viewbank Av. EH19: Bonn 5K 41
Viewbank Dr. EH19: Bonn 5J 41
Viewbank Rd. EH19: Bonn 5H 41
Viewbank Vw. EH19: Bonn 5J 41
Viewcraig Gdns.
EH8: Edin 3J 21 (4H 5)
Viewcraig St.
EH8: Edin 4J 21 (4H 5)
Viewfield EH19: Bonn 5K 41
Viewfield Rd. EH14: J Grn 5G 31
VIEWFORTH 5E 20
Viewforth EH11: Edin 5E 20
EH32: Port S 3H 15
Viewforth Gdns. EH10: Edin 6F 21
EH33: Tran 1G 27
Viewforth Pl. EH30: S Q'fry 2G 7
Viewforth Rd. EH30: S Q'fry 1G 7
Viewforth Sq. EH10: Edin 6E 20
Viewforth Ter. EH10: Edin 6E 20
EH33: Tran 2G 27
Viewpark Gdns. EH19: Bonn 5H 41
Villa Rd. EH30: S Q'fry 1G 7
Violet Ter. EH11: Edin 6C 20
Vivian Ter. EH4: Edin 7C 10
Vogrie Cres. Sth.
EH23: Gore 6F 49
Vogrie Pl. EH23: Gore 6F 49
Vogrie Rd. EH23: Gore 7F 49
Vorlich Cres. EH26: Pen 7E 44
Vue Cinema 2J 21 (1G 5)

W

Waddell Pl. EH6: Edin 6E 12
Wadingburn La. EH18: Las 4F 41
Wadingburn Rd. EH18: Las 5E 40
Wakefield Av. EH7: Edin 1F 23
Walker Cres. EH22: Dalk 4K 41
Walker Dr. EH30: S Q'fry 1F 7
Walker Pl. EH18: Las 7E 40
Walkers Ct. EH14: Edin 4G 31
Walkers Rigg EH14: Edin 3G 31
Walker St. EH3: Edin 3E 20
Walkers Wynd EH14: Edin 3G 31
Walker Ter. EH11: Edin 4E 20
Wallace Cres. EH25: Rosl 2A 46
Wallace Pl. EH33: Tran 1G 27
WALLYFORD 4K 25
Wallyford Ind. Est.
EH21: Wall 4A 26
Wallyford Station (Rail) 3K 25
Wallyford Toll EH21: Muss 2K 25
Walter Scott Av. EH16: Edin 3B 34
(not continuous)
Wanless Ct. EH21: Muss 2F 25
Warden's Cl. EH1: Edin 5E 4
WARDIE 4J 11
Wardie Av. EH5: Edin 5K 11
Wardieburn Dr. EH5: Edin 4J 11
Wardieburn Pl. E. EH5: Edin 4J 11
Wardieburn Pl. Nth.
EH5: Edin 4J 11
Wardieburn Pl. Sth.
EH5: Edin 4J 11
Wardieburn Pl. W.
EH5: Edin 4H 11
Wardieburn Rd. EH5: Edin 4H 11
Wardieburn St. E. EH5: Edin 4J 11

78 A-Z Edinburgh

Wardieburn St. W.—Whitehill Gro.

Wardieburn St. W.
EH5: Edin 4H **11**
Wardieburn Ter. EH5: Edin 4H **11**
Wardie Cres. EH5: Edin 4J **11**
Wardie Dell EH5: Edin 4K **11**
Wardie Fld. EH5: Edin 4J **11**
Wardie Gro. EH5: Edin 4J **11**
Wardie Ho. La. EH5: Edin 4K **11**
Wardie Pk. EH5: Edin 5K **11**
Wardie Rd. EH5: Edin 5K **11**
Wardie Sq. EH5: Edin 4K **11**
Wardie Steps EH5: Edin 4K **11**
Wardlaw Pl. EH11: Edin 6C **20**
Wardlaw St. EH11: Edin 6C **20**
Wardlaw Ter. EH11: Edin 6C **20**
Wardrop's Ct. EH1: Edin 4E **4**
Warrender Pk. Cres.
EH9: Edin 6F **21**
Warrender Pk. Rd.
EH9: Edin 6G **21**
(not continuous)
Warrender Pk. Ter.
EH9: Edin 6G **21**
Warrender Swimming Cen. 7G 21
WARRISTON **6B** 12
Warriston Av. EH3: Edin 6B **12**
Warriston Cres. EH3: Edin 7B **12**
Warriston Dr. EH3: Edin 6A **12**
Warriston Farm Rd.
EH14: Cur 6J **29**
Warriston Gdns. EH3: Edin 6A **12**
Warriston Gro. EH3: Edin 6A **12**
Warriston Pl. *EH3: Edin 7B **12***
(off Inverleith Row)
Warriston Rd. EH3: Edin 7B **12**
EH7: Edin 5B **12**
Warriston's Cl. EH1: Edin 4E **4**
Warriston Ter. EH3: Edin 6A **12**
Washington La. EH11: Edin 5D **20**
Washington St. EH11: Edin 5D **20**
Waterfall Wlk. EH22: Dalk 3D **42**
Waterfront Av. EH5: Edin 3G **11**
Waterloo Bank EH26: Pen 3D **50**
Waterloo Pl. EH1: Edin . . .2H **21** (2F **5**)
EH33: Elph 6F **27**
Waterloo Rd. EH33: Tran 4H **27**
Water of Leith Walkway
*EH3: Edin 1F **21***
(off Malta Ter.)
Water's Cl. *EH6: Leith 5F **13***
(off Shore)
Water St. EH6: Leith 5F **13**
Watertoun Rd. EH9: Edin 1J **33**
Watson Cres. EH11: Edin 6D **20**
Watsonian FC **1C** 32
Watson's Bldgs. EH4: Edin 6C **10**
Watson St. EH26: Pen 2C **50**
Watt Gro. EH22: May 1G **49**
Watt Pk. EH22: Newt 2D **48**
Watt's Cl. EH21: Muss 2D **24**
Wauchope Av. EH16: Edin 7E **22**
Wauchope Cres. EH16: Edin 7E **22**
Wauchope Ho. EH16: Edin 1F **35**
Wauchope Pl. EH16: Edin 7E **22**
(not continuous)
Wauchope Rd. EH16: Edin 7F **23**
Wauchope Sq. EH16: Edin 7F **23**
Wauchope Ter. EH16: Edin 7E **22**
Waugh Path EH19: Bonn 5K **41**
Waulkmill Dr. EH26: Pen 3D **50**
Waulkmill Loan EH14: Cur 2G **37**
Waulkmill Rd. EH26: Pen 2D **50**
[illegible]
Waverley Bri.
EH1: Edin 3H **21** (3E **4**)
Waverley Ct. EH19: Bonn 6J **41**
Waverley Cres. EH19: Bonn 6J **41**
Waverley Dr. EH19: Bonn 6J **41**
Waverley Pk. EH8: Edin 2A **22**
EH19: Bonn 6J **41**
EH22: May 7F **43**
Waverley Pk. Ter. EH8: Edin 2A **22**
Waverley Pl. EH7: Edin 2A **22**
Waverley Rd. EH19: Bonn 6J **41**
EH22: Dalk 3B **42**
Waverley Steps EH1: Edin 3F **5**
Waverley St. EH22: May 1F **49**
Waverley Ter. EH19: Bonn 6J **41**
EH22: May 7F **43**
Weavers Knowe Cres.
EH14: Cur 7B **30**
Webster's Land EH1: Edin 5C **4**
Wedderburn Ter.
EH21: Muss 4F **25**
Wee Brae EH18: Las 4G **41**
Weir Ct. *EH11: Edin 2F **31***
(off Sighthill Bank)
Weir Cres. EH22: Dalk 3A **42**
Well Ct. EH4: Edin 3E **20**
Wellflats Rd. EH29: Kltn 2B **16**
Wellhead Cl. EH30: S Q'fry 2J **7**
Wellington Cotts. EH22: Dalk . . .7B **24**
Wellington Pl. EH6: Leith 6F **13**
Wellington St.
EH7: Edin 1K **21** (1J **5**)
Well Wynd EH33: Tran 2H **27**
Wemyss Gdns. EH21: Wall 3A **26**
Wemyss Pl. EH3: Edin . . .2F **21** (2B **4**)
EH32: Port S 3G **15**
Wemyss Pl. M.
EH3: Edin 2F **21** (2A **4**)
Werberside M. EH4: Edin 6H **11**
Wesley Cres. EH19: Bonn 6K **41**
W. Adam St. EH8: Edin . . .4J **21** (5G **5**)
W. Annandale St. EH7: Edin 7C **12**
W. Approach Rd.
EH11: Edin 5B **20** (6A **4**)
Westbank EH4: Edin 6B **10**
Westbank Loan EH15: Port 2G **23**
Westbank Pl. EH15: Port 2G **23**
Westbank St. EH15: Port 2G **23**
W. Barton Ter. EH4: Edin 2B **20**
West Bow EH1: Edin 4G **21** (5E **4**)
W. Bowling Grn. St.
EH6: Edin 5D **12**
W. Brighton Cres. EH15: Port . . .3G **23**
W. Bryson Rd. EH11: Edin 6D **20**
Westburn Av. EH14: Edin 4E **30**
Westburn Gro. EH14: Edin 4E **30**
Westburn Middlefield
EH14: Edin 4E **30**
Westburn Pk. EH14: Edin 4F **31**
W. Cairn Cres. EH26: Pen 1C **50**
W. Caiystane Rd.
EH10: Edin 6E **32**
W. Camus Rd. EH10: Edin 6E **32**
W. Carnethy Av. EH13: Edin 7J **31**
W. Castle Rd. EH10: Edin 6E **20**
W. Catherine Pl. EH12: Edin 4C **20**
West Cherrybank EH6: Newh . . .4B **12**
West Coates EH12: Edin 4C **20**
W. Colinton Ho. EH13: Edin 6J **31**
W. College St.
EH1: Edin 4H **21** (5F **5**)
West Ct. EH4: Edin 2A **20**
EH16: Edin 1E **34**
WEST CRAIGS **5B** 18
W. Craigs Av. EH12: Edin 5B **18**
W. Craigs Cres. EH12: Edin 4B **18**
W. Craigs Ind. Est.
EH12: Edin 4B **18**
West Cft. EH28: Rat 2E **28**
W. Cromwell St. EH6: Leith 4E **12**
West Crosscauseway
EH8: Edin 5J **21** (7G **5**)
West End **4A** 4
West End EH2: Edin 3F **21** (4A **4**)
West End Pl. EH11: Edin 5D **20**
Wester Broom Av.
EH12: Edin 6E **18**
Wester Broom Dr.
EH12: Edin 6E **18**
Wester Broom Gdns.
EH12: Edin 6E **18**
[illegible]
EH12: Edin 6E **18**
Wester Broom Pl. EH12: Edin . . .5E **18**
Wester Broom Ter.
EH12: Edin 6E **18**
Wester Cl. *EH6: Newh 3C **12***
(off Newhaven Pl.)
Wester Coates Av.
EH12: Edin 4C **20**
Wester Coates Gdns.
EH12: Edin 4C **20**
Wester Coates Pl. EH12: Edin . . .3C **20**
Wester Coates Rd.
EH12: Edin 4C **20**
Wester Coates Ter.
EH12: Edin 4C **20**
Wester Drylaw Av. EH4: Edin . . .7E **10**
Wester Drylaw Dr. EH4: Edin . . .7D **10**
Wester Drylaw Pk. EH4: Edin . . .7F **11**
Wester Drylaw Pl. EH4: Edin 7E **10**
Wester Drylaw Row
EH4: Edin 7F **11**
WESTER HAILES **4F** 31
Wester Hailes Cen.
EH14: Edin 4G **31**
Wester Hailes Pk.
EH14: Edin 4G **31**
Wester Hailes Rd.
EH11: Edin 3E **30**
EH14: Edin 3E **30**
Wester Hailes Station (Rail) . . .**4F** 31
Wester Hill EH10: Edin 4C **32**
WESTER MILLERHILL **5K** 35
Western Cnr. EH12: Edin 4K **19**
Western Gdns. EH12: Edin 4A **20**
WESTERN GENERAL HOSPITAL
. . . .**1C** 20
Western Harbour Breakwater
EH6: Newh 2C **12**
Western Harbour Dr.
EH6: Newh 3C **12**
Western Harbour Pl.
EH6: Newh 2C **12**
Western Harbour Way
EH6: Newh 2C **12**
Western Pl. EH12: Edin 4A **20**
Western Ter. EH12: Edin 4A **20**
Wester Row EH14: Cur 3A **30**
Wester Steil EH10: Edin 3C **32**
W. Fairbrae Cres.
EH11: Edin 1G **31**
W. Fairbrae Dr. EH11: Edin 1G **31**
West Ferryfield EH5: Edin 5J **11**
Westfield Av. EH11: Edin 6A **20**
Westfield Bank EH22: Dalk 4A **42**
Westfield Ct. EH11: Edin 6A **20**
EH22: Dalk 4A **42**
Westfield Dr. EH22: Dalk 4A **42**
Westfield Gro. EH22: Dalk 4A **42**
Westfield Pk. EH22: Dalk 4A **42**
Westfield Rd. EH11: Edin 6B **20**
Westfield St. EH11: Edin 6B **20**
Westgarth Av. EH13: Edin 6K **31**
W. Gorgie Parks EH14: Edin 7A **20**
W. Gorgie Pl. EH14: Edin 1A **32**
W. Grange Gdns. EH9: Edin 1H **33**
W. Granton Access
EH4: Edin 6G **11**
EH5: Edin 4G **11**
W. Granton Rd. EH5: Edin 4F **11**
Westhall Gdns. EH10: Edin 6F **21**
W. Harbour Rd. EH5: Edin 3H **11**
EH32: Cock 3F **15**
W. Holmes Gdns.
EH21: Muss 2D **24**
Westhouses Av. EH22: May 1G **49**
Westhouses Dr. EH22: May 1G **49**
Westhouses Rd. EH22: May 1G **49**
Westhouses St. EH22: May 1G **49**
W. Ingliston Cotts. EH28: Ing 5D **16**
Westland Cotts. EH17: Edin 7E **34**
West Loan EH32: Pres 6D **14**
W. Loan Ct. EH32: Pres 6D **14**
W. Lorimer Pl. EH32: Cock 4F **15**
W. Mains Rd. EH9: Edin 2J **33**
W. Maitland St. EH12: Edin 4E **20**
West Mayfield EH9: Edin 7K **21**
W. Mill Bank EH13: Edin 6J **31**
W. Mill Ct. EH18: Las 4G **41**
W. Mill La. EH4: Edin 3E **20**
W. Mill Rd. EH13: Edin 6H **31**
Westmill Rd. EH18: Las 5G **41**
[illegible]
W. Montgomery Pl.
EH7: Edin 1K **21**
Westmost Cl. *EH6: Newh 3B **12***
(off Pier Pl.)
W. Newington Pl. EH9: Edin 6J **21**
W. Nicolson St.
EH8: Edin 4J **21** (6G **5**)
W. Norton Pl.
EH7: Edin 2K **21** (1K **5**)
WESTPANS **1K** 25
W. Park Pl. EH11: Edin 5D **20**
W. Parliament Sq. EH1: Edin 4E **4**
W. Pilton Av. EH4: Edin 6F **11**
W. Pilton Bank EH4: Edin 5F **11**
W. Pilton Brae EH4: Edin 5G **11**
W. Pilton Cres. EH4: Edin 5E **10**
W. Pilton Crossway EH4: Edin . . .5F **11**
W. Pilton Dr. EH4: Edin 5F **11**
(not continuous)
W. Pilton Gdns. EH4: Edin 5F **11**
W. Pilton Grn. EH4: Edin 5F **11**
W. Pilton Gro. EH4: Edin 5F **11**
(not continuous)
W. Pilton Lea EH4: Edin 5F **11**
W. Pilton Loan EH4: Edin 5F **11**
W. Pilton March EH4: Edin 4G **11**
W. Pilton Pk. EH4: Edin 5F **11**
W. Pilton Pl. EH4: Edin 5G **11**
W. Pilton Ri. EH4: Edin 5F **11**
W. Pilton Rd. EH4: Edin 5G **11**
W. Pilton St. EH4: Edin 5F **11**
W. Pilton Ter. EH4: Edin 5F **11**
W. Pilton Vw. EH4: Edin 6F **11**
W. Pilton Way EH4: Edin 5G **11**
West Port EH1: Edin 6C **4**
EH3: Edin 4G **21** (6C **4**)
West Powburn EH9: Edin 1J **33**
W. Preston St. EH8: Edin 6J **21**
West Princes Street Gdns.
. . . .**3F** 21 (**4B** 4)
West Register House **3A** 4
W. Register St.
EH2: Edin 2H **21** (2E **4**)
W. Register St. La.
EH2: Edin 2H **21** (2E **4**)
W. Relugas Rd. EH9: Edin 1H **33**
W. Richmond St.
EH8: Edin 4J **21** (6G **5**)
W. Savile Rd. EH16: Edin 1K **33**
W. Savile Ter. EH9: Edin 1J **33**
W. Saville Gdns. EH9: Edin 1J **33**
W. Shore Bus. Cen.
EH5: Edin 3F **11**
W. Shore Rd. EH5: Edin 4E **10**
W. Shore Rd. Trad. Est.
EH5: Edin 3F **11**
Westside Plaza EH14: Edin 4F **31**
W. Silvermills La. EH3: Edin 1F **21**
W. Stanhope Pl. *EH12: Edin 4C **20***
(off Stanhope Pl.)
West St. EH26: Pen 3C **50**
West Telferton EH7: Edin 2F **23**
West Ter. *EH30: S Q'fry 1G **7***
(off High St.)
West Tollcross
EH3: Edin 5F **21** (7B **4**)
West Werberside EH4: Edin 6H **11**
West Windygoul EH33: Tran 3F **27**
W. Windygoul Gdns.
EH33: Tran 4F **27**
West Winnelstrae EH5: Edin 6J **11**
West Woods EH4: Edin 7H **11**
Westwoods Health Club **7H** 11
Wheatfield Gro. EH20: Loan 5A **40**
Wheatfield Loan
EH20: Loan 4B **40**
Wheatfield Pl. EH11: Edin 6B **20**
Wheatfield Rd. EH11: Edin 6B **20**
Wheatfield St. EH11: Edin 6C **20**
Wheatfield Ter. EH11: Edin 6B **20**
Wheatfield Wlk. EH20: Loan 5A **40**
Wheatsheaf La. EH22: Dalk 1C **42**
Whinny Loan EH21: Wall 4B **26**
EH33: Tran 4B **26**
Whin Pk. EH32: Cock 4F **15**
Whin Pk. Ind. Est.
EH32: Cock 4F **15**
Whins Pl. EH15: Port 3G **23**
WHITECRAIG **7G** 25
Whitecraig Av. EH21: Whit 7G **25**
Whitecraig Cres. EH21: Whit . . .7G **25**
[illegible]
Whitecraig Gdns. E.
EH21: Whit 7G **25**
Whitecraig Rd. EH21: Whit 7G **25**
Whitecraig Ter. EH21: Whit 7G **25**
White Dales EH10: Edin 7G **33**
Whitehall Ct. EH4: Edin 1K **19**
White Hart St. *EH22: Dalk 2C **42***
(off Buccleuch St.)
Whitehead Gro. EH30: S Q'fry . . .2H **7**
WHITEHILL **4H** 43
Whitehill Av. EH21: Muss 3C **24**
(not continuous)
Whitehill Bus. Cen.
EH22: Dalk 3G **43**
Whitehill Dr. EH22: Dalk 3F **43**
Whitehill Farm Rd.
EH21: Muss 4C **24**
Whitehill Gdns. EH21: Muss 4C **24**
Whitehill Gro. EH22: Dalk 3F **43**